PRAYERS FOR LIFE'S PARTICULAR MOMENTS

Dorothy McRae-McMahon

Published in Great Britain in 2001
Society for Promoting Christian Knowledge
Holy Trinity Church
Marylebone Road
London NW1 4DU

British Library Cataloguing-in-Publication Data

A catalogue record for this book is available from
the British Library

ISBN 0–281–05297–2

Typeset by Pioneer Associates, Perthshire
Printed in Great Britain by
The Cromwell Press, Trowbridge

Contents

Introduction	v
Using these Liturgies	vii
Worship	viii
CELEBRATING	1
The Joy of Water	3
Litany of Hope	6
Celebrating Christmas	7
Transfiguration	10
Celebrating, Sending Out and Blessing	13
Turn to God, Rejoice in Hope	15
Celebrating the Life Among Us	19
Celebration of the Coming to Age	21
Celebrating the Years	25
Praise to the Evangel	28
PAUSING TO REFLECT	31
Jesus Prays Through the Night	33
In the Stillness, In the Silence	34
Easter Meditation	37
Meditation on the Journey of Jesus Christ to Death and Life	39
The Gathering of Grief	40
FAITHFULNESS	45
Offering All We Have	47
The Beckoning God	50
Christmas	52

On the Road   56
The Sacramental Meal   59

REMEMBERING WHO WE ARE   63
All Saints' Day   65
Taken By the Hand   67
At Home With God   70
The World – A Sacred Space   73
Turn Away From Death   75
Tenants in God's Household   78
Invited to the Feast   81

NEEDING SUPPORT   85
Just Walking By   87
Survival of the Vulnerable Good   90
It's Not Easy   93
Service of Prayer and Concern for Outworkers   96
For the Uprooted Ones   99

WITH THE WIDER COMMUNITY   103
Missing Persons   105
Honouring the Outworkers   108

OCCASIONAL PRAYERS   111

Introduction

The liturgies in this book have been written for many different situations and people. As we journey through life, we celebrate, we struggle, sometimes we need support or we pause to reflect, we remember who we are and we are sometimes joined with people outside the church community.

Sometimes we are people in Sunday morning worship. The theme for the day comes from the journeying with God of the biblical witnesses to faith.

Sometimes the liturgy arises from a time on the way when things are hard or when a time in life is honoured and respected and there is cause for celebration. As I faced becoming older myself, I decided that the 'coming to age' was such a time. Age, especially in Anglo-Celtic cultures, is so often only ritually noticed when we die.

Some of these liturgies are for the community beyond the Church. I have always felt that one of the gifts that the Church could give unconditionally to the wider community is its skill in creating rituals. If I say 'unconditionally' it is because I observe that the Church often uses such occasions for its own purposes – sneaks in a bit of religion as a marketing ploy or as a sort of conscience activity. In my experience, if we give with generous grace, people often then ask us to bring in something of our God. If we insist on our God being there as our price for the gift, it is less likely to be received.

Two of the liturgies come from experiences around the World Council of Churches Assembly in Harare in 1998 when I was Moderator of its Worship Committee. The liturgies, however, do not arise from the assembly itself so much as from the people who surrounded us in that assembly, the painfully and joyfully surviving people of Zimbabwe and from Nelson Mandela as he visited with us.

Another is a joint effort by myself and a group of homeless women. I had been asked to speak at a dinner for homeless women which was being organized by a New South Wales government staff person who was working on the prevention of violence against women. I found myself anxiously wondering what I would say to these women. After thinking of a few stories about gifts I had received in relating to some of the women who live on the streets of Sydney, I decided that maybe I could plan a simple ritual to honour their journey. On the night I found myself seated at dinner with a prostitute, a young woman who had run away from a violent husband, a transgendered woman and a woman who was struggling with drug addiction. We had a rather astonishing dinner conversation during which they decided that I was rather innocent and not very streetwise. They told me horror stories of their experiences in church-run hostels for the homeless where the church demanded that they attend worship or Bible study three times a week in return for a bed and where one of them had been sexually abused by a 'Christian' staff member. Then they asked for my autograph 'in case I might be important one day'!

At the end of this, I said I had better prepare for a little ceremony that I was planning. 'Oh!' they said with enthusiasm. 'We like things like that. We will help you get ready.'

They looked at my liturgical 'props'. 'Ah,' they said, 'clearly this long cloth is a red carpet for us.' They draped it up a nearby staircase. 'This candle is a light in the window of the home we might one day find and we could put it at the end of the red carpet inside this nice little glass jar.' Then they looked at the smaller candles and said, 'Maybe these are the little lights on the way when something good happens to us and we could put them here and there on our red carpet.' By this time I was in tears and they asked, 'Why are you crying, reverend?' Why, indeed? They had recognized and developed my liturgy and claimed it for themselves. They had given it more symbols of hope than I would have ever dared to offer them from my privileged life.

I knew again that liturgy has a life of its own if we will set it free among the people as they walk their way on the journey of life. When it comes in Spirit and in truth it will be owned and recognized and used for the enhancing of life. Almost all of these liturgies have been prepared for specific moments in the lives of particular people. Most effective contemporary liturgy is prepared like this, in my experience. You may like to take some ideas that are here and create your own liturgy for you and your place and situation.

Dorothy McRae-McMahon

Using these Liturgies

Most of these liturgies would benefit by the inclusion of music. I have left it for the users to decide what music they will add. Music is a very cultural thing, even in the Church these days. There are now very few 'well-known hymns'!

At the beginning of each liturgy, I have noted the main resources that would be needed for the symbolic images or acts already written into the liturgy. I always assume that people add their own ideas about preparing the environment for liturgical events – that they will bring in their own cloths, candles, crosses, banners, contextual images or symbols, or anything else that might enhance the moment.

When a liturgy has been specifically prepared around certain Bible readings, those readings are included, otherwise it is assumed that people will select their own as appropriate. Having said that, some of the services that are attached to certain readings may well be used in other contexts and with other readings.

Worship

Worship is a circle of wholeness,
the integration of creation with its source,
the intertwining of spirit with Spirit
in a sense of oneness,
stretching down the ages
and on into distance.

It is as concrete as touching your hand
and as mystical
as the heart of the Divine –
a grounding in the essence of humanity
and a wide sweep into timeless spaces,
renewing in grace,
confronting in holiness
and always made valid in love.

Celebrating

We celebrate this God
who leaps free of all our boundaries
in love stretching out from horizon to horizon,
and in mercy bending deep
into fragile human hearts.

THE JOY OF WATER
A tribute to the Widows' Association of Harare

For this service you will need

- *Jugs of water*
- *A bowl of salt water*

OPENING SENTENCES

Claim the joy of water for the poor of the earth!
Let it flow and pour and sprinkle for all the people!

Call for the rivers to be shared
and the rain from the heavens
to gather in great ponds of mercy,
that all may know each day the gift of God in water.

Jugs of water are carried to the table

SONG

STORY

At the University of Harare for the World Council of Churches Assembly in 1998, the student residence in which some delegates stayed was cleaned by the normally unemployed women of the Widows' Association. Night and day they cleaned the corridors, the rooms and the bathrooms, working long hours for very little pay. They were welcoming women, kindly to the delegates as visitors to their city. Each day the delegates went off to their meals and the WCC meetings and left them to do the cleaning. One morning a delegate returned to get something from her room in the middle of the morning. As she approached the bathroom nearby, she heard unusual noises – ecstatic noises, sounds of happiness, with much laughter and some singing. She looked in the door and there were the cleaning women, clutching tiny fragments of soap, bathing and showering in joy and delight. They were lifting up their arms to feel the water flowing over their bodies, almost dancing under the showers and lying back in the full bath in bliss, encouraging each other in this wondrous moment of access to running water. When they saw her, the sounds suddenly stopped and then they all laughed together, celebrating the moment and her recognition that they had 'seized their day' against the odds.

GRIEVING

We grieve, O God, who gives us water for all life,
that so many of us have only hard-won drops to drink,
while others of us have access to water at every turn
and often waste it with careless abandon.
Forgive us, O God.

We grieve that we rarely even think of this,
that we take the water we have for granted
with little care for others.
Forgive us, O God.

Connect our hearts with those whose tears of grieving
are shed in their need and fear for their thirsty children.
Let us dip a finger in this water and taste the tears of the world,
sharing in its grieving and all its thirsts for justice.

A bowl of salt water is passed among the people while a silence is kept

ASSURANCE

Jesus Christ is our living water,
pouring forth grace towards us who grieve for what we have done.
Open your hearts to receive the life of Christ
and the renewing of grace for this day and the next.
We are forgiven.
Thanks be to God!

READINGS

POEMS ABOUT WATER

SONGS AND PICTURES ABOUT WATER

DOXOLOGY

COMMITMENT

We will need the living water of God for our task in the world.
O God, we pray for this water, that we may be your faithful servants.

Silent prayer

As we are restored by your gifts, these are our hopes for the world:

*The particular hopes relating to work being done by the
people are shared*

We will carry the love of God into the four corners of the earth.
**We are the people of God, brought to birth in the rush of
   water,**
washed and sustained day by day in the beauty of water.
We see the wonder of the rivers and streams,
and the endless waves of the mighty seas.
Our faces are lifted up to receive the gentle rain
and the miracle of the greening of the earth as it falls.
**In all this, O God, we give thanks for your endless gifts
   to us**
**and commit ourselves to move for the just sharing of them
   with others.**

Let us give to each other water for this journey
and commit ourselves to care for each other on the way.

The people pour water into each other's cupped hands

Praise to you, God of all creation!
Praise to you for the gift of water!
Amen.

MUSIC OR SONG

BLESSING

We are blessed for ever by the poured out life of Christ.
Let us go and pour this blessing over the heads of all the people.
And may the streams of living water flow beside the road as you go,
the warmth of the love of God move within you
and the Spirit be found in the ripples of grace around you.
Amen.

LITANY OF HOPE

This litany can be accompanied by a miming of the images and the lifting up of symbols representing each image. It can also be expanded by reading the relevant Bible passages in between each section of the litany.

You will need

- *A bowl of earth, some seeds and a jug of water*
- *A dead branch and a branch with leaves*
- *A candle to light*

As we rejoice in hope, let us remember our salvation:
The river of our tears
will become a well of living water.
The seed which falls into the ground
will rise and bear much fruit.
Hallelujah!

The crushed and bowed down
will be lifted up in God's embrace.
The dead trees of our parched life
will spring forth again in healing leaves.
Hallelujah!

Our turmoil and commotion
will be held in the hollow of God's hand,
and our journey in the darkness
will be led by the flame of God's love.
Hallelujah!

We are not alone.
We are surrounded by a great cloud of witnesses.
Amen! Amen!

This litany was first written for part of the Closing Worship at the World Council of Churches Assembly in Harare, 1998.

CELEBRATING CHRISTMAS

For this service you will need

- *Advent candles already lit*
- *An unlit 'Christ candle' with taper for lighting*
- *Small candles for lighting during the intercession (watch the spacing of these as they can generate much heat!)*

CALL TO WORSHIP

In the beginning was the Word,
and the Word was with God:
light of life for all the people.

The word was with God,
and the Word was God:
full of grace and truth.

The word became flesh and lived among us,
giving us the power to become children of God.
**Glory be to God,
the God of the ages of ages.**

PRAYER OF INVOCATION

Surprise your people, O God, with the joy of your birthing of love
    among us.
Break past the boundaries of our full rooms and into the holy
    spaces near to us.
Call to us from afar, that we may search and find your dwelling
    place.
Come to us here, on this day of celebration.
Amen.

The Christ candle is lit among the Advent candles

CAROL

CONFESSION

God of the Incarnation, flesh of our flesh, gentle God in the
    humble manger:

If we have forgotten what it means to expect your coming
in the face of so many absences of love and goodwill,
forgive us, O God.

Silent prayer

If we have lost our hope in your sounds of joy abroad in the world,
reinforcing our lack of faith with cynicism and apathy,
forgive us, O God.

Silent prayer

If we have given over Christmas to children,
as though adults are past the wonder and mystery of surprises,
forgive us, O God.

Silent prayer

Carry us again to the place of your birth that we may see your face
and believe.
Amen.

ASSURANCE

Joy to the world, the Christ has come!
And the coming is for all the people who will receive this gift of God.
Fall to your knees before the Christchild and then rise up in hope
and faith!
Amen.

CAROL

READINGS

SERMON

PRAYER OF THANKSGIVING

Let us bring our prayer of thanksgiving to God:

Thanks be to God, that our doubts and fears
cannot stop the birth of God among us.
Thanks be to God that Jesus comes among ordinary people,
all sorts of people!
Thanks be to God that this Good News
has carried down the ages to us from that first Christmas,
that we may share in the blessing of this day.
Amen.

CAROL

PRAYERS OF INTERCESSION

God, who sent to us the child of grace,
we know that because we lift up this day as a day of love and joy,
we make it the hardest day of the year for those who have little
    of that.
The very hope that we proclaim
becomes a burden and grief for those whose hope is low.
Even as families gather to share in the celebration,
there will be many for whom celebration is a mockery and a
    painful pretence.
We light these small and flickering candles
for all those who cannot claim this day in truth.

*The people light the small candles and, if they choose, name particular
people or groups*

Dear God, these small lights are as fragile as the life you chose to
    enter in vulnerability.
Give us the faith to believe that, even in frailty,
the signs of love will be abroad in all the earth today.
Amen.

CAROL

COMMISSIONING AND BLESSING

Turn to God – the God of the cross and the crib.
Rejoice in hope!
Love lies waiting in the womb,
the womb of the faithful one.
Love lies waiting for a place to be born among us, even us.
Come, prince of peace.
Come, Jesus Christ.

May the song of the heavens sound in joy around us,
the star shine forth in the shadows of the earth
and the dream for the world be born in our hearts again today.
Amen.

TRANSFIGURATION
Celebrating when we have seen the Christ
in a new way

This service is especially suitable for ecumenical use.

For this service you will need

- *A table in the front or down the central aisle covered in paper to absorb any ink*
- *A length of cloth stretched across the table and flowing onto the floor (with paper under it to protect the carpet or floor)*
- *Felt pens for writing names on the cloth*

SILENCE

GREETING

Blessed is God always,
now and ever and to the ages of ages.
Amen.

O God, open my lips,
and my mouth will declare your praise.

Create in me a clean heart, O God,
and put a new and right spirit within me.

Do not cast me away from your presence,
and do not take your Holy Spirit from me.

Restore to me the joy of your salvation,
and sustain in me a willing spirit.
(Psalm 51.15, 10–12)

SONG

CONFESSION

If we have believed that we have seen
the only Christ and all of Christ:

Forgive us and open our eyes,
O God who is beyond our seeing.

When we believe that the word
is only heard in truth in our own church:
Forgive us and open our ears,
O Spirit who is beyond our knowing.

If we have stopped looking for you
in surprising places and with unexpected people:
Forgive us and open our hearts,
O Christ, who is beyond our imagining.

READING
Matthew 17.1–9

RESPONSE TO THE WORD
Let us remember those who have revealed to us a new vision
    of the Christ,
especially those who belong to churches other than our own.
Let us write their names on this cloth.

The people come forward and write the names

O God, we give thanks for all these people whose lives have
    revealed you to us.
May we take the gifts of life that they have given to us and offer
    them to others.
Amen.

AFFIRMATION
Let us affirm our faith together:

We believe in a God
who is never confined to our imagining,
is never in bondage to our beliefs,
and never held fast in our dwelling places.

Our God is the mystery
of divine and human bound together,
of power and vulnerability,
of crucifixion and resurrection.

Our God is the wonder of truth and compassion,
of liberation and responsibility
of eternal wisdom and costly grace.

We celebrate this God
who leaps free of all our boundaries
in love stretching out from horizon to horizon,
and in mercy bending deep
into fragile human hearts.

COME DOWN THE MOUNTAIN WITH US

Come down the mountain into our life, Jesus Christ.
Come and join our world
and lift up hope among us.

The people name the places that need hope

For these, who we have named,
and for those who we hold in the silence of our hearts,
we pray, gracious God.
Come, Jesus Christ, and give courage to your church,
uniting us in love and faith, that the world might believe.
Renew a right spirit within us, O Christ.

Come, Jesus Christ,
and inspire in us a new vision of your life,
a new commitment to justice and peace
flowing from your word into the world.
We turn to you.
We rejoice in hope.

THE LORD'S PRAYER
(each in our own first language)

SONG

BLESSING

May the Christ be revealed in wonderful ways,
may our eyes be opened to see this blessing
and our faith be lifted up in joy.
Amen.

CELEBRATING, SENDING OUT
AND BLESSING
For a departing colleague or group member
who has worked for justice

For this service you will need

- *A wine glass chosen as a gift for the person leaving, filled with good wine or the person's favourite drink*

OPENING SENTENCES

We are here to give thanks for faithfulness,
this faithfulness and all faithfulness:
For God has given us gifts of faithfulness.

We are here to celebrate the gift of ministry,
this ministry and all ministry:
For God has given us gifts for ministry.

We are here to ask a blessing on the future,
this future and for all that lies before us:
**For God has given us the gift of hope,
a hope that will carry us into a new day.
Thanks be to God!**

DOXOLOGY

CONFESSION

Gracious God,
God who walked our way in Jesus,
we have not always been able to receive
all that was offered in this ministry.

Person leaving:
**And I have not always been able to give
all that you hoped from me.**

For we are your humble human people,
and we are no longer searching for the Messiah among us.

Even as we fail, the victory has already been won for us
and grace, justice and peace is abroad in all the earth.
For Christ has died,
Christ is risen
and Christ will come again!

READING
Isaiah 25.1–10

GIVING THANKS

What are the qualities which we value in the life of (*Name*)?

The people offer words which describe those qualities

O God, for all these things which we find in (*Name*),
our friend and colleague, we give you thanks.
In this service to you and the church,
we have experienced your hand upon us,
wiping away the tears of life,
lifting the shroud from the people in love and justice.

We have seen in (*Name*) one who gives all that he/she has
in the preparing of your feast for the little and the least.
We are joined today by the unseen presence of those
with whom she/he has stood in many places.
For this we give thanks.
We celebrate his/her life as she/he has followed the Christ.

THE SENDING OUT AND BLESSING

Let us gather around (*Name*)
and send him/her forth into God's new day.

The people gather around the person

What are the gifts we ask of God for this new day?

The people name the gifts

(*Name*), we send you out in the power of the Spirit.
We send you out in love, our love and the love of Christ.
We send you out in faith with a God who is faithful for ever.
Go and continue to be part of the transforming of the world.

A cup of wine is given to the person

Carry the wine of life into all the corners of the earth.
But first, stay still for a time our friend, rest in the peace of Christ.
Drink this wine yourself.
This time the wine and the feast are for you.
Amen.

GENERAL BLESSING

Go in peace,
go as though we too are the people of the feast.
And may God's table be spread before us,
Christ Jesus be our host
and the Spirit lead us into the dance of life.
Amen.

The party follows

TURN TO GOD, REJOICE IN HOPE

This service is especially suited for ecumenical use.

For this service you will need

- *A pot of earth*
- *A large branch with leaves*

GREETING

The peace of Christ be with you.
And also with you.

CALL TO WORSHIP

Turn to God:
**Sacred centre of the universe,
eternal mystery of grace.**

Turn to God:
**The one whose footsteps mark the way
on the journey into life.**

Turn to God:
**And hear the songs of freedom
sung deep in the heart of the world.**

Turn to God, rejoice in hope!
It is right to bring our thanks and praise!

SONG

CONFESSION
Why do we not turn to you, God of grace?
You created us with the dignity of freedom
and we go our way as if we do not need you.
You offered us the gift of the whole creation for our home
and we consume its hospitality
with ungrateful disregard.

You gave us each other for our neighbours
and we build our citadel estates
and defend our gates as though we never met.
You called us into being your one church
and we have failed to sit at table,
even when you are the host.
Why do we not turn to you, O God?
**If we look upon your face,
we will know who we are.**

Silent reflection

Christ have mercy.

Sung: **Kyrie eleison.**

ASSURANCE OF PARDON
Look without fear, people of God.
In the cross of Christ,
we see revealed the life of the New Covenant
which is given for all
for the forgiveness of sin.
In the Spirit, we will receive grace upon grace.
Gloria, Gloria.

THE ENTRY OF THE WORD

The Gospel

Acclamation

SONG

AFFIRMATION OF FAITH

In response to the word, let us affirm our faith:

There is God,
creating out of our nothingness
a vision of a new heaven and a new earth.
breaking forth beyond our horizons
in an eternal sunrise of justice, peace and grace.
This is our God, rejoice in hope.

There is God,
rising in our gatherings
with nail-torn hands held out
in earthly credibility,
bearing the marks of our deathly pain,
the cost of the resurrected life.
This is our God, rejoice in hope.

There is God,
Holy Spirit, living in all the earth
as though truth is the possible ground of our being,
turning the shadow of a cross
into a shelter for our resting
on the way to life lived in passionate freedom,
until the whole creation
sings again in praise of its Maker.
This is our God, rejoice in hope.

INTERCESSION

We will plant the life of your cross,
the victory of your rising,
on the ground of our life, O God.

Your love for the world
marks all creation as sacred space
for the fullness of your life.
Lift up your risen life in us, O God,
that all the earth may see and believe.

A branch is raised and planted in a pot of earth

We will carry the life of your cross
among the bowed-down ones,
that they will turn and see in us
the joining of their life with yours
in the passion for justice,
in the power of truth,
and love which rises in victory.
Lift up your risen life in us, O God,
that all the earth may see and believe.

The branch is lifted high

We will carry the life of your cross
into the church, O God,
among our separations,
that all may one day see in us
the miracle of your power to make us one,
the bright colour of our journey
lived in the richness of the Spirit
and courage born of faith in your grace.
Lift up your risen life in us, O God,
that all the earth may see and believe
that the Christ has come.
Amen.

The branch is placed among the people

SONG

BLESSING

Go in peace into all that this day brings.
We go in faith and hope.

And may the face of God be turned towards you,
the hand of Christ be stretched out to hold you
and the Spirit be found as wisdom within you.
Amen.

CELEBRATING THE LIFE AMONG US
For people working together

For this service you will need

- *A variety of flowers arranged on a cloth on the floor or on the table in the centre*

GREETING

Peace be with you.
And also with you.

OPENING SENTENCES

Life rises in our midst:
sometimes hard-won life.

It surprises us when it blossoms forth at unexpected times:
and in unexpected places.

It comes with power stronger than death:
life born of faithfulness,
life born of courage,
life born of God.
Thanks be to God.

SONG

SOMETIMES WE MAKE IT HARD FOR LIFE

Sometimes, God of life, we do things that make it hard
for the best of life to live among us.
We crush it with our lack of hope,
we fail to affirm it when we see it begin to grow in its fragility,
we destroy it with exploitation and injustice,
we can't imagine it coming from some people
or we fail to give it support
because our own life is low and we resent it in others.
Forgive us when we make it hard for life to live, O God.

Silent reflection as a flower is crushed

ASSURANCE

God, in Christ Jesus, is the life that rises
from the depths of all our failure, pain and grief.
This life is never defeated!
Thanks be to God!

Sung twice: **Hallelujah.**

READING

Isaiah 35

Silent reflection

AFFIRMATION OF LIFE AMONG US

Let us look at each other and see qualities and gifts which
contribute to life among us. Without naming anybody, let us say
the gift or quality, and taking a flower from the table, hold it as a
sign that we have received this blossoming of life.

The people do so

Let us affirm the life among us:

**We affirm that we see and experience
this life in our midst.
It invites other life in us,
it gives life to people beyond us.**

**We affirm that here in this place
life can be sustained,
that in us new life can emerge and grow
and that hope for life
is to be cherished every day.**

**We celebrate the God who conquered death.
We hold ourselves open to a new creation in us.
We believe that in every child of God
the Spirit breathes a thousand, thousand gracious possibilities.**

PRAYERS FOR OUR LIFE

God of new life,
we pray that you will care tenderly for the life here.
We pray that the work we do will bring life to others

beyond this place,
especially in places where it is hard for life to survive.

Silent reflection

We give thanks for the life we experience in each one of us
and we pray that the way we live and work together
will encourage that life.
Let us pray for each one:

*Each person says, in turn, the name of the person on their left, beginning
with the leader*

We are glad to be here with each other.
**We commit ourselves to go on in this year,
trying to care for each other,
giving and receiving in a sharing of gifts and graces,
that we may be part of the transforming life of God.
Amen.**

SONG

BLESSING
Go into the year in faith.
And may each day be born of God,
each hour be a journey with Christ
and each moment be filled with the grace of the Spirit.
Amen.

CELEBRATION OF THE
COMING TO AGE

For Christian older people who wish to
celebrate their own lives

For this service you will need

- *A central table prepared with a long cloth placed across it and trailing
  down towards where people are seated*

- *To the left of the cloth four candles – one large white candle and smaller gold, purple and yellow candles*
- *To the right of the cloth a variety of flowers loose on the table*

OPENING

We are the people whose lives have spanned the decades,
the people who have seen the greatest changes in history.

The gold candle is lit

We are the people who have walked through the valleys
and climbed high in the mountains of living.

The purple candle is lit

We are the people of the dignity of years,
the wisdom of experience,
and refining in the fire of life.

The yellow candle is lit

**We are those who have come to age
and we are loved and respected by God.
God is with us still.**

The large white candle is lit

SONG

LET US REMEMBER

Let us remember the hardest things for us,
the changes which have been most challenging,
the deaths of many things we valued
and the deaths of people along the way,
the struggles for survival,
the confusions and ambiguities,
the traumas and pain for us and in the wider world during our lives.

Silent remembering

Let us share the times or people we have remembered
and place flowers on the cloth to honour this part of our life.

The people come forward, name their memory, take a flower from the table and place it on the cloth. Some may call out their memory while another places the flower

PRAYER

Dear God, you have travelled with us through this time.
We place in your loving hands all these memories from our past.
We ask you to heal them,
and to make them more gentle within us.
Grieve with us and feel with us, O God.
Claim your presence among these our journeys
and lay them kindly to rest.
Amen.

MUSIC OR SONG

READING

Bible readings or poems or meditations that people have written.
Telling of local stories – stories about the lives of people or events
that are significant in that place.

MUSIC OR SONG

CELEBRATION OF WHO WE HAVE BECOME

If the group is smaller, this can be done seated in a circle for all to hear

Let us pause, look respectfully at ourselves and at each other.
In the silence, decide what it is that you celebrate in yourself – a
quality, gift, or talent.
If the person next to you is known to you, decide what you most
respect in that person.

Silent reflection

Now turn to each other and share what it is that you respect in
yourself and the other person.

The people share with each other

We are each people of great worth.
Together we are enough to transform the world!
Let us call out the qualities, gifts and talents we have discovered
among us.

The people call out the things they have shared with each other

PRAYER

Gracious God, we so often doubt that we are people of worth.
Today we have remembered who we are,

and all that you have created and sustained in us.
We thank you for your life in us,
your wisdom and courage, your love and faithfulness.
We celebrate a great possibility: that in the days of our ageing,
in strength and in frailty, in sickness and in health,
we can still be your people,
called to be part of the bringing in of your reign, called to be
    your church.

Either:

**We are the people of the feast. The table of celebration is laid
    for us.
We share a common cup of life and break a common loaf of
    salvation.
Thanks be to God!**

Followed by Holy Communion

Or:

**We are the people of the feast.
Our lives are due for celebration!
We have come to age.
Thanks be to God!**

Followed by a party

DOXOLOGY

BLESSING

Go in faith, as you have done so often before.
Go in love, as you have been faithful in loving others.
Go in peace, the peace which is beyond understanding,
and may God go with you,
the God who has never left you nor forsaken you over the years,
the God who travels with you until the end of time,
your Creator, Sustainer and Redeemer.
Amen.

CELEBRATING THE YEARS

For a congregation wishing to celebrate the lives of older people

For this service you will need

- *A long piece of purple or red cloth, with paper to put underneath it to protect the carpet or floor*
- *Felt pens for writing on the cloth*

GREETING

The peace of Christ be with you.
And also with you.

CALL TO WORSHIP

God of all time,
God for whom eternity is but a moment:
We worship you.

God who trod our life
in all its harshness and all its beauty:
We worship you.

God who is the wisdom of the ages,
Spirit of all truth, healer and comforter:
We worship you.
We give you thanks for all our years with you.

SONG

RECEIVING OUR LATER YEARS

Dear God, if as older people
we have decided to stop growing
and die before our time,
with no expectation that you will call us on
to new adventures of living and growing:
Forgive us.

If we have seen ourselves as of little worth,
holding our learning and wisdom to ourselves,

believing our witness to the faith journey
is too ordinary to share:
**Forgive us and restore us as your royal children
and honoured friends.**

If we, as younger people,
have regarded older people as having little to give:
Forgive us and open us to their gifts.

ASSURANCE

Hear the word of assurance:
Nothing in all creation can separate us
from the love of God in Christ Jesus.
Rise up and live!
Amen!

READINGS

SERMON

Suggestions:
Stories of faith given by older people.
Stories of faith about the lives of older people.

SONG

CELEBRATION OF FAITHFULNESS

Let us remember those, our older people
who have prepared the way for the Gospel over the years.

*The cloth is spread like a pathway down the centre of the church – with
the paper underneath*

People of quiet daily faithfulness,
people who did the things that no one else wanted to do,
people who were little recognized,
people of wisdom and courage,
people who cared for others,
the ones who never gave up and who gave much,
the people who were the living stones of this church,
with Jesus Christ as their foundation.
Let us write their names on this cloth:

The people write the names in felt pen

Let us gather around this cloth and sing the Doxology.

COMMITMENT TO COMMUNITY

The older people gather at the front of the church or stand in a circle around the younger people, possibly wrapping the cloth around them, and say:

We will cherish you,
the young in the faith.
We will guard you as those
who have already walked the way before you.
We will encourage you with the wisdom of experience.
We will open our hearts to the new insights which come
      from you
and will hold you fast with our love and hope.

The younger people stand or turn to the older people and lift the cloth high, and say:

We will cherish you, those who are older in the faith.
We will respect you as those who have already walked
      the way before us.
We will celebrate the strength of your life-tested faith
and we will build on that with our gifts
from a God who goes on calling us to new things
which even now are breaking from the bud,
in our lives and in yours.

A SERVICE OF HOLY COMMUNION
(Optional)

SONG

BLESSING AND DISMISSAL

Go in peace,
and may the God of grace be found as grace in you
the God of faithfulness be seen in the strength of your faith
and if your feet are old and your knees trembling,
may the dancing Spirit take your hand in joy.
Amen.

— 27 —

PRAISE TO THE EVANGEL

For this service you will need

- *A symbol of creation – e.g. flowers, rocks, a branch, a plant*
- *A gold cloth*
- *A large candle*
- *A number of smaller candles*
- *A cloth to write on and felt pens (optional)*

OPENING SENTENCES

Praise to God who calls us down the ages:
The one who has always been the source of our life.

A symbol of the creation is placed on the table

Praise to God who dances within our life:
The Spirit of grace, the Spirit of truth.

A gold cloth is swirled around the table

Praise to God the Evangel:
**The one who calls to us by name,
who saves us and brings us to abundant life,
Jesus, the Messiah, the Christ.**

A large candle is lit

SONG

IT IS NOT EASY

Even though our hearts are filled with gratitude,
even though our lives sometimes break into new blossoming
because we travel with you, Jesus Christ,
we come before you in our anxious frailty
when we hear your call to be your witnessing people.

A silence is kept

How will we share the Good News in a hard time?
When will we find the right words?
Where will we point to a truly welcoming community?
Is our faith enough to share?

A silence is kept

Forgive our lack of courage, O God.
**Forgive our lack of overflowing joy in the spreading of
your word.**

ASSURANCE OF PARDON

Hear the words of assurance:
Jesus has walked this way beside us.
There is nothing in all creation
that can separate us from the love of God.
Thanks be to God!

READINGS
Suggested
Isaiah 25.1–10
John 1.35–51

SONG

SERMON

AFFIRMATION OF FAITH
**God, our God, is the Creator,
who forms new things from nothing,
even our emptiness.**

**God, our God, is the Christ,
who would rather die than leave us without grace,
who sits with sinners and walks with the searching,
who brings hope and healing
from as little as a touch of his robe.
Christ's arms stretch out to embrace us all
and to carry us beyond where we thought we could go
in costly risen life.**

**God, our God, is the Holy Spirit,
giver of the gifts we need,
discovered in surprising places,
always moving towards us
in healing, comfort and love.**

PRAYERS OF INTERCESSION

We come before you with empty hands, O God,
held out to you in hopeful expectation
that we will be given the gifts
for the task of being the bearers of your gospel.
These are the gifts for which we long, O God:

The people name the gifts they need or write them on a cloth

We already see some gifts among us
and we light these small candles
in celebration of the signs of hope around us:

The people name any signs of hope and light the candles

We thank you for these signs, O God.
**Fan the small flames of brave, clear life in us,
for we are your people and you are our God.
Amen.**

SONG

BLESSING

Go in faith, go into the world.
And may the Word be discovered within us,
the Spirit take wings in freedom before us,
and may we be held in the hollow of God's hand.
Amen.

Pausing to Reflect

There is a God
at whose feet we may sit,
and gathered there is love.

There is a quiet space for safe encounters
and wiser understandings for our learning,
a robe for the touching of our hand
to share healing grace
from the body of the Christ.

JESUS PRAYS THROUGH THE NIGHT
Prayers for the end of the day

For this service you will need

- *A cross and a candle*

GREETING

Come into this place in faith, sisters and brothers,
for all the earth is a dwelling place for God.

A silence is kept

Come into this moment in hope, brothers and sisters,
for Jesus prays through the night.

A silence is kept

Come into this space in gentleness, sisters and brothers,
for in the Spirit have we all received grace upon grace.

A silence is kept

The circling of life has entered its resting place,
the invitation to peace.
We turn to God. We rejoice in hope.
This cross and this candle are signs of God's faithfulness.

BEFORE OUR GOD

As we turn to you this night, O God,
if there are issues in our lives
which cause us to lower our eyes
and to cover our faces in the light of your presence:
Forgive us.

If we as your churches
have been a faltering witness to your love:
Forgive us. We wait in faith for your renewal.
Amen.

LITANY FOR THE ENDING OF THE DAY

The ending of the day
is a heartbeat of silence in the life of God:
for our pausing,
for the laying down of the weight of our concerns.

The going down of the sun is a misting of the sharpnesses:
for our easing,
for the kindly covering of the unbearable questions.

The coming of the darkness
is the touch of God on tired heads:
for our resting,
for the facing of tomorrow when it comes,
tomorrow which is the day of faith and hope. Amen.

BLESSING

Go into the night in peace,
and may the God of eternity stretch out the heavens above you,
the God of each earthly moment be closer than breath
and the Spirit cover you with warm bright wings.
Amen.

IN THE STILLNESS, IN THE SILENCE
Sitting at the feet of Jesus with Mary

GREETING

Peace be with you.
And also with you.

CALL TO WORSHIP

In the companionship,
in the loving presence

in the unspoken:
there is eternal care and wisdom.

In the silence,
in the stillness,
in the spaces:
there is God.
Let us worship God.

SONG

BE STILL

Be still and know that I am God.
You call to our bodies, minds and souls, O God,
and we move and think our feverish thoughts.
We stir anxiously around in the depths of our souls.
In this brief moment, O God,
we will imagine what it would mean to be still
and sit in trust at the feet of the Christ.

Brief silence

What would need to cease in order to make space for this moment?

The people share what would have to stop, or reflect in silence

Let us keep the space and the silence together.

A silence is kept

Maybe in the silence there is a music for us,
A new music of love and healing.

Music

God comes to us in Spirit and in truth.
God covers us with warm wings of grace,
taking our hand for the journeys into this our new day.
Amen.

READINGS
Amos 8.1–12
Colossians 1.15–28

SONG

THE GOSPEL
Luke 10.38–42

SERMON

THE AFFIRMATION OF FAITH
In response to the word, let us stand and affirm our faith:

There is a God
at whose feet we may sit
and gathered there is love.
There is a quiet space for safe encounters
and wiser understandings for our learning,
a robe for the touching of our hand
to share healing grace from the body of the Christ.

There is a place
near to feet that have walked our dusty ways
and moved in courage among our complexities,
felt our painful choices at the crossroads,
turned themselves reluctantly towards our harder paths
and formed footsteps ahead of us
towards a truer, braver, many-coloured life.
We will sit at the feet of our God.

SONG

WHO WILL WE GATHER TO US?
Who will we call to sit with us at the feet of Jesus Christ?
Who waits for this gracious space,
for more love, more justice, more hope?

The people gather in those for whom they pray and a silence is kept

Lay your hands on the heads of these, our sisters and brothers,
    O God.
Give them the gift of a sacred pausing moment,
a linking with the quiet strength of your love.

Sung twice: 'Jesus, remember us, when you come into
your kingdom' (*Taizé*)

Gather us all into your presence, Jesus Christ:
**that we may be renewed and sustained
in the week to come.
Amen.**

OFFERING

SONG

BLESSING

Go without fear into the silences,
go in peace.
And may God the loving parent be your womb-space,
God in Jesus Christ bring you to new birth
and the Spirit sing songs of joy to welcome you.
Amen.

EASTER MEDITATION

This meditation was first written for a performance of Haydn's Seven Last Words of Christ *at the Sydney Opera House.*

For this meditation you will need

- *A bowl of earth and some seeds*
- *An empty glass bowl*
- *A long red cloth*
- *A large jug of water (and small glasses if you choose)*

I THIRST

After this, when Jesus knew that all was now finished, he said (in order to fulfil the Scriptures) 'I am thirsty'. A jar full of sour wine was standing there. So they put a sponge full of the wine on a branch of hyssop and held it to his mouth.

(John 19.28–29)

WE THIRST

We thirst,
like vulnerable seeds
waiting under the parched farmland earth
for the rain to release us to life.

Seeds are placed on a bowl of dry earth

A silence is kept

We thirst,
like the ones who grieve the loss of loves
in the deathly betrayals
which leach away the waters of hope.

An empty bowl is placed in the centre

A silence is kept

We thirst,
like a nation longing for the generosity of its old soul
as it watches its life drying up and dying in meanness.

The people share their particular longings for their country

A silence is kept

We thirst,
like those whose spirits fly free in truth
while their bodies groan and weep in the bleeding
from the costliness of the flight.

A long red cloth is placed

A silence is kept

We thirst,
not for the sweet easy drink of denials,
nor for sour wine offered by those who would call us from our path,
but for the holy water of risen life.

A jug of water is placed in the centre

A silence is kept

*Water from the jug is shared around the group – poured into cupped
hands or passed in small glasses*

Go in peace,
go in grace,
go as those who walk with the Christ who also thirsts.
Amen.

MEDITATION ON THE JOURNEY OF JESUS CHRIST TO DEATH AND LIFE

Voice 1:
God who soon will die, let us pour the perfume of flowers on
  your head.
May we walk with you towards risen life?

Silence

Voice 2:
The way is not always clear to us.

Voice 1:
God who soon will die, let us pour the perfume of flowers on
  your head,
and walk with you towards risen life.

Silence

Voice 2:
We stand in this place at the time of the passion and wonder.
Would we call out 'Jesus, look at me, I know who you are'?

Voice 1:
God who soon will die, let us pour the perfume of flowers on
  your head.
We long to walk with you.

Silence

Voice 2:
We work in this place wanting to believe that God will set us
  free to live
and that we can share this message with others.

Voice 1:

God who soon will die, let us pour the perfume of flowers on
   your head.
We pray that we will walk with you.

Voice 2:

God, welcome us to your side,
let us know the power of your grace,
let us know our place in your story,
help us to know the truth of the gospel.

Give us courage to find healing,
to smell the warmth of the candle,
your light among us,
and know that we are your children.
Amen.

THE GATHERING OF GRIEF
For use on Good Friday or on another occasion of grieving

*To occasionally gather up all the grief among a community and focus it
in a liturgical event is healthy. Good Friday may be only one day for this
to occur.*

For this service you will need

- *A piece of red cloth for tearing*
- *A bare dead branch*
- *A large candle*
- *Small bowls of fragrant oil*

OPENING SENTENCES

Grief, grief, through all the universe the tears fall like the rain:
and we add our own grieving.

Grief, grief, the cries of the people sound among their painful
   struggles:
and we add our own cries.

Grief, grief, the Christ, the one who bleeds, whose life is poured out, joins the grieving in Godly vulnerability:
and we touch the wounds of this Christ born of our own frailty. We will stay here for this hour.

SONG/MUSIC

WE CAN HARDLY BEAR TO SEE

O God, we can hardly bear to look at what lies around us.
The pain of humankind and the faltering creation itself is
     too much for us.
The people are fleeing our wars and violence.
There is rape and torture, children lost and abused,
hate and rejection of those who are different,
starvation and cruelty,
with huge powers of oppression standing between us and justice.
What will we do?
Who will save us from ourselves?

A silence is kept and a red cloth is torn and placed in the centre

O God, we turn away from the wonder of this planet
which you gave to us for our well-being.
It groans and struggles for survival.
There is desecration of the land,
and destruction of the forests.
The air is sick, the waters are dying.
The precious creatures which you gave to us for company
gasp and die in distress.
How can we restore the earth?
When will we be reconciled with all around us?

A silence is kept and a bare dead branch is carried to the centre

O God, our own lives carry the wounding of life.
We are bowed down by things which seem too much for some,
while others seem to go free.
We grieve for our losses in illness and death,
in separation and alienation from each other.
We reel under hard choices
and the dreadful burden of our mistakes.
We sadly see where we have been on this journey
and long for a new way before us.

— 41 —

Who will understand this our life?
Who will comfort and forgive us?

A silence is kept

THIS IS THE TIME OF WAITING

Three days of waiting.
Three moments of waiting.
Three thousand, thousand years of waiting for an end to the
  grieving of the people.

READING

REFLECTION

WE ARE JOINED BY THE CHRIST

Hear the words of assurance:
See, touch the wounded hands, put your hand in the bleeding
  side of the Christ.
This, our God, lives within our grieving and even our dying.
Come, place all your grieving alongside the heart of Christ.
Christ have mercy.

A large candle is lit and small bowls of fragrant oil are placed nearby

WE BELIEVE

God is present in the tomb of our waiting,
creating the costly miracles of the victory of good,
of love, of grace, of the restoration of all things.

In the centre of our waiting
the seeds of our salvation are announced in small signs,
in small kindnesses, in humble courage,
in lives of fragile hope, in faithfulness.

God is not defeated.
Life is more powerful than death.
This we believe.
From this will we live.

OUR GRIEVING IS GATHERED INTO THE LIFE OF GOD

There will be beauty for ashes and the oil of joy for mourning.
There will be oil for our cherishing and oil for our healing,
oil for our anointing and oil for our calling to the task.

A silence is kept

While we sing quietly or listen to music, you are invited to anoint the
hand of a person near to you. Each person may choose whether to
name silently or openly a particular grieving at this time.

The bowls of oil are passed among the people

Let us pray:
God of eternity, in faith we leave these our grievings with you.
We will walk forward to a new day,
the day of rising life.
We will sing our songs of hope where hope is hard to find.
Great is your faithfulness to us, O God of the ages of ages.
Amen.

SONG

BLESSING AND DISMISSAL

Go in peace.
Go with a gift of kindness in your hearts.
And may God the loving parent hold you firm,
God in Jesus Christ be there to meet you
and the Spirit cover you with gentleness.
Amen.

Faithfulness

On the road we find our God walking alongside
as though knowing where we are going,
travelling with our questions and fears,
opening for us wisdom,
from one who knows the journey,
who has never really left the road of life
for the greener fields of heaven.

OFFERING ALL WE HAVE
For people beginning a significant task

For this service you will need

- *Five small loaves or bread rolls*
- *Two fish or pictures of fish*
- *Symbols of the task that is being begun*

OPENING SENTENCES
Each from our own places,
the people are coming together.
And God is with us.

Leaving all but our lives behind,
we come with empty hands.
And God is with us.

We come to meet the Christ,
to know our Maker in a new way,
to wait for the leading of the Spirit.
God is with us and God will be with us.
We will make our offering to God.

Small loaves and fishes are placed in the centre

SONG

WE HAVE NOTHING HERE
O God, as we watch the people come to sit at your feet,
waiting for healing, waiting for the Word,
we hear you say again to us,
'They need not go away, you give them something to eat.'
And we have nothing here
but five loaves and two fishes.

Silent reflection

We know the hard life that lies here before us.
We know the struggles that are already taking place,
the woundedness and hunger in the souls of the people.
And we have nothing here
but five loaves and two fishes.

Silent reflection

This is a deserted place and the hour is now late.
How can our small offering
be enough to feed the longing people, O God?
For we have nothing here
but five loaves and two fishes.

Silent reflection

THE ASSURANCE

Have faith, have hope!
As we place our humble offering
into the hands of the Christ, the people will be fed.
This is the word to us.
Hallelujah!

READING

Matthew 14.13–21

THE OFFERING

In response to the word,
this is the moment to place into the hands of God
all that we have prepared.

Symbols of the task are placed on the table

This is our work, O God.
It is never enough, but we offer it in faith to you.

We also offer ourselves, O God,
Our small gifts and graces,
our frail lives and hopeful hearts.

The people say what they will try to bring

This is who we are, O God.
We are never enough, but we offer ourselves in faith.

PRAYER OF INTERCESSION

Let us pray for the expanding of our offerings.
What do we need for this day?

The people say what they believe is needed

We will never know all that is needed.
Take even our prayers, gracious God,
and add to them your gifts of wisdom, of knowing,
a vision beyond our sight.

Sung: **Kyrie eleison.**

LITANY OF EXPECTATION

Bring them all, bring each of them.
Bring offerings to the Christ!
**The grass will become a resting place for the people,
the heavens will pour down a blessing upon us.**

Even in the breaking, new gifts will be given,
touched and transformed by the hands of our God.
Made new to our eyes,
returned into our waiting hands as healing,
as nurturing and cherishing,
as a feast enough for all.
We will eat and be filled!
We will share the good things together!
**We will take up what is left over and carry it forth into
    the world**
in overflowing love and kindness.

We will see that our nothing is enough,
that there is always more than we knew
if we turn to God and rejoice in hope.
This is the day that our God has made.
We will rejoice and be glad in it!
Amen!

SONG

BLESSING

The task is before us,
a moment of opportunity for the grace of God,
the entry of love into the world yet again.
Go forth into this day in peace.
And may the God of all time, the God of the ages of ages,
the Triune God,
be among us, around us and within us
this day and for evermore.
Amen.

THE BECKONING GOD
For those about to begin a brave conversation together

For this service you will need

- *A symbol of new life – buds, new leaves, or a baby*
- *A cross*
- *A long cloth to represent a pathway*
- *A red cloth or scarf to represent bleeding on the way*
- *A basket of coloured paper arrows*

GREETING
The peace of Christ be with you.
And also with you.

OPENING SENTENCES
You beckon the whole universe into life, O God.
You, who are the source of all that is, our Creator.

A symbol of new life is placed on the table or lifted up

You beckon us to follow you on your costly journey, O God.
You, who are the Christ, our Way, our Truth, our Life.

The cross and 'pathway' cloth are placed on the table and down onto the floor

You beckon us still into new birthings, O God.

The sign of bleeding on the way is placed on the table

You, who are Holy Spirit, our nurturer, our lover, our friend.
Let us worship God!

SONG

BEGINNING A BRAVE CONVERSATION

In all honesty, O God,
we would sometimes not open a conversation with you,
or with each other.
It is easier to pretend we do not hear, see or feel your invitations.

Silent reflection

The shadowlands of our old standing places feel safer to us
than the light of new possibilities,
or the colours of your dreams for us.

Silent reflection

But do not stop calling to us,
God of our pilgrim journey.
Beckon us on into your brave conversations,
and open our hearts to the newness in each other, O God.
Forgive our lack of courage and hope.

Sung: 'Bless the Lord, my soul' (*Taizé*)

ASSURANCE

The word to us in Christ is that we are never left alone,
    nor forsaken.
Let us walk this journey together in faith.
Amen.

READING

Isaiah 42.5–9

REMEMBERING PAST BRAVE CONVERSATIONS

*The people are asked to take an arrow from the basket, say the name of
the person whose brave conversations have led to their new life, and
place the arrow on the pathway*

THANKSGIVING AND INTERCESSION

Let us give thanks and offer our future to God.
Thank you, God, for our past:
and all those who have beckoned us towards your life.

Thank you for our present:
with its small callings, its stirrings in our souls,
its flashes of truth and its soundings towards love.

Make clearer your voice in the midst of the clamourings,
conceive in us a fresh growing of love
and nourish it within our being so that it comes forth in freedom.
Live in risen life in our midst, O God.

Thank you for our future:
before we know it, before we see it, before we enter it,
in faith, we invite you to beckon us on, O God,
that we may be your people
and you may be our God.
We commit ourselves to you
as we enter this time and place
and our brave conversations together.
We will risk hearing each other,
trust ourselves to each other in faith
and await the presence of your Spirit among us, O God.
Amen.

BLESSING

Go in peace to delight in the offerings of your Creator,
tread a safe and costly path with the Christ walking before you
and ride high with the wings of the Spirit as your cover and
    your flight.
Amen.

CHRISTMAS
A time of giving

For this service you will need

• *A large bowl of flowers*

GREETING

The grace and peace of Christ be with you.
And also with you.

OPENING SENTENCES

God has joined our living!
The gift of the Christchild is among us.
Come in joy to worship our God!

Mary has been faithful!
She has given her body in labour and pain
to bring this child into the world.
Come in joy, as faithful humankind shares in the birthing!

This is the day of giving and loving.
This is the day when the bud breaks forth
as the blossoming of the life of God in our midst.

A large bowl of flowers is carried to the centre

This is Christmas Day!
Let us join the songs of welcome to the infant Jesus Christ!

CAROL

CONFESSION

Dear God,
Sometimes our growing life shrivels up
in fear of not having enough for ourselves.
We become half-alive, convinced that everything is scarce.
We limit our capacity to share.
Our generosity, our compassion,
and our commitment to justice dries up and almost dies within us.
Forgive our smallness of heart, O God,
and bring us to life again as we receive your gift of love
in Jesus Christ.

ASSURANCE OF PARDON

Love has come into the world,
a free gift of grace for ordinary people,
a nurturing of hope,
and a promise of new things!
Thanks be to God!
From the Spirit have we all received, grace upon grace.

READINGS

CAROL

SERMON

AFFIRMATION OF FAITH

In response to the word, let us stand and affirm our faith:

**We believe
that God has entered the flesh of our life in Jesus Christ.
Today we celebrate that we are honoured
as worthy to carry the Child of God into the world.
Today we hear the song of hope
from within ourselves and among us,
a hope that peace and love will survive,
a joy that this will be for all people.**

**Today we see the world with new eyes,
with the eyes of a loving God.
We see that each of us is linked with the life of God.
We hear the cries of the world
and believe that each voice
comes to us like the cry of a child in Bethlehem.**

**In faith we lift our hearts,
in faith we will tend the seeds of hope
for the people of the earth.
We will cherish the weak,
suckle the thirsty, cover the cold
and gather in the lonely,
because Christ is within us
and love and life are born again among us.**

CAROL

PRAYERS OF INTERCESSION

God of love, as we celebrate this day,
and welcome you as the Christchild,
we share gifts with each other as a sign of the rebirthing of
    your love.
We remember those who still wait for the signs that you
    have come.
They wait for justice.

They wait for your promise of peace and goodwill
to be brought to life among them.
These are the people who we especially remember today.
We long for them to share fully in your living giving.

*The names of people from particular countries and situations are
mentioned and flowers from the bowl are placed on the communion
table or altar*

Add to each small beginning of our life, O God:
as you did in Bethlehem.

Gather us towards the wonder of your love, O God:
as you gathered the shepherds.

Call us on with a star of hope before us:
as you called to those who were wise long ago.

For we would be faithful like Mary and Joseph:
**that the child of freedom and grace
may be born among us again and again.
Amen.**

THE LORD'S PRAYER

THE OFFERING

This is a moment when we share our life that others may receive life.
The bowl which we fill for others
is taken by them and goes on
in flowing gifts of life beyond our imagining.
It also will become filled with flowerings of life for us
because we have shared in the generous life of God.

The offering is received

Life has blossomed in us,
in response to the love of God for all people!

Children distribute gifts of flowers from the bowl among the people

CAROL

Go in peace,
for this is the gift of God to us all.
And may the God who spoke to an ordinary woman
speak in your life,
the God who came as a vulnerable child
touch you in your vulnerability,
and the Spirit join you in songs of joy.
Amen.

ON THE ROAD
Our road and the Emmaus road

For this service you will need

- *A loaf of bread*

CALL TO WORSHIP

Journeying on the road, before we reach our home:
You find us and join us, O Christ.

Within our anxious musings, between our sadder longings:
You find us, O Christ.

There in the brokenness, there in the nearness of our heartspace:
You find us and join us, Jesus Christ.
Let us worship our God.

SONG

CONFESSION

It is a strange thing, O God,
that we often go on searching around the tombs of life to find you,
hunting through the empty spaces,
returning to the deathly moments,
asking among the hostile places and people,
insisting on trying to find you in distant theories and doctrines
as though you would make it hard for us.

Silent reflection

We place upon you our own contrariness,
our own manipulations,
our own distancing from those we love.
We punish ourselves as we punish others,
forgetting your kindly grace towards us
and all frail and humble people.

Silent reflection

Forgive us, O God.
Forgive us, and reveal to us the nearness of your presence.

ASSURANCE OF PARDON

Hear the word of pardon to us from a Jesus who stayed with
    the people
who longed for him.
Hear the word of grace from the One
who invites us always to break the bread in an eternal covenant
    of love.

A loaf is placed on the table

We are forgiven.
Thanks be to God!

READINGS
Psalm 116.1–4, 12–19
Acts 2.14a, 36–41

SONG

THE GOSPEL
Luke 24.13–35

SERMON

AFFIRMATION OF FAITH
In response to the word, let us affirm our faith together:

**On the road we find our God walking alongside
as though knowing where we are going,**

travelling with our questions and fears,
opening for us wisdom,
from one who knows the journey,
who has never really left the road of life
for the greener fields of heaven.

In our minds we find our God,
lifting the veil from mysteries,
calling us away from easy fantasies,
joining us on our way,
measured step by honest step,
looking reality in the face,
in the counting of the cost of risen life.

In our hearts we find our God,
responding to our need
for company which stays towards the night,
sharing our table
and taking the things we know
in hands which break and bless
and give all that we need
for the lifting of our lives in hope.

PRAYERS OF THANKSGIVING AND INTERCESSION

Let us offer each other a piece of bread.

The bread is passed around

Hold the bread in your hand and imagine that, as you do this,
you are able to ask Jesus Christ about something that concerns you.
In the silence make this your prayer to God.

The people make their prayers in silence

Let us eat this bread, believing that Jesus is with us.
Who in the world at this time
waits for the bread of life and the love and justice of God?
Who cries out for answers to their fears and suffering?

The people name those who suffer

O God, we pray that you will be found on the road with all
    these people,
walking with them in their fear, sharing their suffering,

and staying with them until the night.
May we share the bread of life with them in your name.
Amen.

SONG

BLESSING AND DISMISSAL

We leave this hour in the company of God.
May we always know this,
may we always trust this
and may we always find the Christ
in the breaking of bread.
Amen.

THE SACRAMENTAL MEAL

*I once saw a man eat a meal as though it was a sacrament. He was
from Zimbabwe.*

For this service you will need

● *Baskets of fruit, bread and nuts*

OPENING SENTENCES

Food, food – costly, free, generous nurturing:
For all of us, for all.

Food, food – unexpected gift, prepared with love:
For all of us, for all.

Food, food – set before us as an invitation to gather around the
    table together.
Bread of life, bread for the world.

SONG

A TRUE STORY

He sat with his meal before him on the table, not a greedy meal, even though he had served himself from the buffet.

I sat opposite with my meal before me, thoughtlessly gathered from the supply on the side tables, and opened my mouth to begin a conversation with him as a possible new friend.

Then I saw that his eyes were fixed with wonder on his plate as he looked reverently at the food which was there. After some moments, he lifted his fork and slowly, carefully, took a mouthful of food. He raised his eyes and gazed thoughtfully into the distance as he chewed – with a deep and solemn joy, a fleeting smile passed across his face at intervals as he savoured each taste, each fragment of food, as though he was storing it up for the future. After each mouthful was finished he surveyed his plate in wonder again and made a careful selection of the next mouthful until the food was gone. He sat before his empty plate in meditative silence and then respectfully left the table.

I knew I was seeing a man eating a meal as though it was a sacrament. He was eating as one who had never seen such food before and knew that, after the Assembly of the World Council of Churches, he might never do so again.

I looked at my meal. It looked different. The world looked different. The sacred meal of Jesus Christ would always look different.

PRAYER OF CONFESSION

Many of us never look at our food, O God.
Sometimes we look at it as though we are due for it,
or consider that it is not as we wanted it to be.

Silent reflection

Sometimes we wish we had more when we have enough
and do not notice the empty plates of others.

Silent reflection

Sometimes we eat it quickly as though it has no significance
in order to hurry on to more important things.
Even when it is the meal at your Holy Table, O Jesus Christ,
we often take it for granted.

Silent reflection

Forgive us, forgive us, O God.
Forgive us when we know not what we do.
Forgive us when we do not see or care.
Forgive us when costly meals become cheap for us.

The eucharistic elements are carried to the table

ASSURANCE

Hear the word to us in Jesus Christ:
I am the bread of life.
Take this bread, take this cup.
It is given for you, even you and all of you.
Thanks be to God!

READINGS

SONG

SERMON

AFFIRMATION OF FAITH

Baskets of fruit, bread and nuts could be carried and placed on the table
between each section of the affirmation and then shared out among the
people later

In response to the word, let us affirm our faith:

The bounty of God the Creator surrounds us with grace,
spread in generous measures of loving creativity,
poured forth for generation after generation
in hopeful abundance,
in an endless invitation to hospitality.

The feasting Christ walks in our scarce life
as though all of us might be part of the celebration,
as though each of us might be a guest at the banquet,
as though we might all be together at the table,
holding each other as precious,
dying before we will give up love
or life which is lived to the full.

The laughing Spirit moves in endless freedom,
stirring, surprising, bestowing gifts as she moves.
Wisdom is foolishly faithful to hope,
eternally living for truth
and never settling for less –
as though we are worth the struggle
and could really be the emerging children of God.

This we believe.
This is the wonder of our God.

PRAYERS OF THE PEOPLE

Who will we gather to our table,
the place of our prayers to God at this moment?
Who is not yet present at the feast of life
because of injustice, oppression, vulnerability and loneliness?
Who have we not noticed because their voices are silenced,
or because we do not think they are worth noticing?

The people bring their prayers for others

O God who calls us all to share the hospitality of your table,
as we remember these your loved children,
call forth in us the same generosity, the same grace, as we find in you.
**In the power of your Spirit, raise up in us a courage for justice,
a commitment to kindness
and the unity for which you long in your church.
In the name of the Christ,
Amen.**

THE EUCHARIST

BLESSING

Go as those whose cup of life runs over.
Go as those who have received the bread enough for others.
And may the fruitfulness of the creation be spread before you,
Christ Jesus host your every meal
and the Spirit fill you with joy.
Amen.

Remembering Who We Are

Hallelujah! Hallelujah!
We are blessed by God!
Thanks be to God!
We are known and seen and still we are blessed.
Thanks be to God!
Jesus sits on the mountain top of life
and gathers us in to the sainthood of all believers.
Thanks be to God!

ALL SAINTS' DAY
The Beatitudes

As a setting for this service, the people could hang around the church ribbons or pieces of cloth or paper carrying the names of those whom they regard as the saints who surround them from the past.

CALL TO WORSHIP

Hallelujah! Hallelujah! We are blessed by God!
Thanks be to God!

We are known and seen and still we are blessed.
Thanks be to God!

Jesus sits on the mountain top of life
and gathers us in to the sainthood of all believers.
Thanks be to God!
Let us worship God.

SONG

CONFESSION

We come before you, O God, in humble confession,
Knowing that you are open to hear us and receive us.
If we have found it hard to bless each other,
in our differences, in our self-righteousness,
remind us of your spirit of overflowing blessing.

Silent reflection

If we have looked at others with a lack of understanding,
if we have failed to notice that some people are carrying burdens
    on the road,
give to us your caring insights, your loving glance.

Silent reflection

— 65 —

If we have not received your blessing of us,
pushing away your gifts of grace
and remaining victims of our own lack of compassion,
forgive us and open our hearts.

Silent reflection

ASSURANCE

Watch and listen. Christ has looked upon us all with love.
Hold the silence before God and wait in faithful expectation
    for the gift of grace.
It is there waiting for us now.
Amen.

READINGS

Revelation 7.9–17
1 John 3.1–3
Matthew 5.1–12

SERMON

THANKSGIVING

God be praised!
As the summer follows the spring,
as the green leaves grow after the fire,
as the sunlight swings from coast to coast,
so the gifts of God have come to us, even us.
As we lift our faces to the rising of the mountains,
the blessings of God spread forth towards each one of us,
the saints of God in this day.
Dear God, we are thankful, we are thankful.
Amen.

PRAYERS OF INTERCESSION

Who will we bless this day
because we have brought them into the presence of God?
Who will we gather at the feet of Jesus Christ for healing
    and comfort?
Who are those who are going through the ordeals of life?

The people say who they are

All-knowing God, pour on these your children
all that they need for survival, renewal and restoration.
Then, dear God, as you blessed the saints of old,
spread out on the plains in humble faith and waiting to be taught,
so come to us, your disciples of today,
and remind us of the possibilities that you see in us.

Silent waiting on God

Speak to us each, in the depths of our souls,
and tell us what you have seen to bless there.
Speak to us, that we may be lifted up in hope
and take up the task as your saints in the world for this day.
We pray in the name of Christ.
Amen.

COMMISSIONING AND BLESSING

We are the saints of God.
We are called to be the church.
Go forth in faith, in hope and in love!
And may the face of God be turned towards us,
the Spirit hover close as our covering of love
and Christ Jesus find us as we long to be found.
Amen.

TAKEN BY THE HAND
Remembering that we are the community of the church

For this service you will need

- *A long cloth to represent a pathway*
- *Outlines of hands cut out in different coloured paper in a basket*
- *A candle*

OPENING SENTENCES

You are our God:
and we are your people.

Walking a chosen pathway:
with Christ who is our Way.

A cloth is placed on the table, flowing onto the floor like a pathway. A basket of hands is placed upon it

Watching for the signs of new things:
in the light of the Spirit of God.

A candle is lit

SONG

THE GRIEVING
Dear God, you give us a dream for our life,
but sometimes it seems too much for us
and we become afraid and tired.

Silent reflection

Sometimes we become absorbed in small things
and fail to notice the great hope to which we are called.

Silent reflection

Sometimes we simply do not know what to do
as we face the world around us.
We grieve our failures, O God.

ASSURANCE
Hear the words of assurance,
for all who come in hope and faith:
I have formed you and called you.
I will take you by the hand.
Behold, I am making all things new.
Thanks be to God!

READING
Isaiah 42.9–5

REMEMBERING
Let us remember those people
who have taken us by the hand
in important moments in our faith journey.

Silent reflection

Turn to your neighbour and share the names
of those who have taken you by the hand.
Then go forward and take a hand from the basket and place it
  around the candle.

The people share and place the hands

THANKSGIVING

Thanks be to God for good and faithful friends.
They have been lights for our journey
and as palm branches spread on our way,
as cups of living water held to our lips,
as healing oil poured on our heads
and as wise ones for our guiding.

DOXOLOGY

(Sung)

OFFERING A HAND TO EACH OTHER

Let us turn to each other and ask for one particular
prayer for the church:

The people share with each other

Now pray for the church as requested.

WE ARE THE CHURCH

We are the church.
I invite you to take the hand of the person to your right and say:
'God has taken you by the hand.
In the name of Jesus, go and be the church.'

SONG

BLESSING

We are always the broken body,
but the word to us in Jesus Christ is that
we are made whole and enough for the task.
Go with the grace of God into this day.
Amen.

AT HOME WITH GOD

CALL TO WORSHIP

You shall love the Lord your God with your whole heart:
Our hearts are warmed in the presence of God.

You shall love the Lord your God with your whole soul:
Our souls lift in the flight to freedom in the presence of God.

You shall love the Lord your God with your whole mind:
There is no wisdom greater than the wisdom of our God.

And you shall love your neighbour as yourself:
Peace be with you!

The people exchange the peace with each other

PRAYER OF INVOCATION

Holy God, we will never deserve your presence with us, but still you
are there for us, like a rock under our feet. Give to us today a clear
awareness of your company, for you are the God of our salvation, the
God whom the people of old have sought and worshipped, as we do
today.
Amen.

SONG

CONFESSION

There are many things that separate us from the worship of God
and from love for our neighbour.
Let us think on these things in the silence of our hearts:

A silence is kept

Let us say aloud some of these barriers to our wholehearted
worship of God:

The people make their confession

It is not easy, O God.
So many things distract us.
In the face of the realities of our life,
we often feel the need to secure our future
in ways which do not depend upon faith in you,
but upon more and more material securities.

Sometimes our neighbour is hard to love
and we are tired of being loving.
Sometimes life itself makes it hard to love you
because we feel you are unjust, O God.
We can't see why we are so wounded and sinned against.
Loving God, please understand our journey
and be with us in forgiveness.
We pray this in the name of Jesus Christ,
Amen.

ASSURANCE

Hear the word to us in Jesus:
Those who have faith will receive grace upon grace.
We are forgiven!
Amen.

READINGS

Deuteronomy 34.1–12
1 Thessalonians 2.1–8
Matthew 22.34–46

SERMON

SONG

AFFIRMATION OF FAITH

Let us celebrate our God:

We celebrate our God,
who is not afraid of our minds
with all their questions,
and all their doubting searchings for the truth.

We celebrate our God,
who knows and loves our deepest hearts,
whose compassion is always greater than ours
so that the measure of our kindness
is always less than that of God.

We celebrate our God,
who engages with our souls,

**linking us with the mystery of the universe,
the endlessness of eternity,
yet is as close to us in our tiny beings
as a parent with a child.**

INTERCESSION

God, who sees far beyond our seeing,
who listens far beyond our hearing
and who speaks to us in the longing hearts of all people
and all creatures,
arouse in us a deep and powerful love for all you have created.
Show us the places where you find a need for your love,
that we may share with you in making this earth a home for all,
a safe and healing place, a peaceful and kindly place,
where justice reigns and flows like a mighty river through the
    whole of life.
Even with our human blindness, we can see some for whom
    your gift, and our gift, of love is needed at this time.

The people share their prayers for others

Even as we pray to you, O God,
we know that we are called to be your friends in this task.
Give to us all that we need in commitment, in unselfishness
and in faithfulness to you to be part of your loving of the neighbour.
We ask this for Christ's sake,
Amen.

SONG

COMMISSIONING AND BLESSING

The God we worship is never confined to this holy place,
so go and travel with the God who is found in surprising places.
Go and take up the adventure of faith in praise of our God.
And may the holy mystery of God be found beside the road,
the wonder of the costly love of Jesus embrace you
and the Spirit bless and keep you always.
Amen.

THE WORLD – A SACRED SPACE

For this service you will need

- *A large candle or a brazier of burning coals*
- *An earthenware bowl*
- *Earth, perhaps brought by the people from where they live*

GREETING
Welcome to this sacred space,
a space where we might come soul to soul with our God.

CALL TO WORSHIP
The burning bush, the flame of the life of God,
which is never consumed:
burns in the sacred ground of this our world.

The flame is lit

The life of Christ, God-with-us, has entered our life:
and declares our humanness as a sacred place.

An earthenware bowl is placed before the flame

The Spirit, the go-between, a melody of connection between us
    and our God:
sounds a song in all the earth until the end of time.
Let us worship our God.

SONG

THE GRIEVING
There, on this God's sacred ground, was a trembling hope:
and we did not see it.

There, like a silent scream, was a cry of longing and loneliness:
and we did not hear it.

There, in awkward self-consciousness, from a culture we did not
    recognize,
was a hand stretched out towards us:
and we did not touch it.

There, deep in the soul of one we met,
was a new understanding of God:
and we failed to respect that soul enough to meet that God.

Silent reflection

God, forgive us:
for we stand in grief on this, your sacred ground.

ASSURANCE

Even the ground of our lives in their grieving and failure
is already occupied by the grace of God.
From the Spirit have we all received, grace upon grace.

READING

SERMON

AFFIRMATION AND INTERCESSION

Let us affirm our faith together:

**We believe that every place
is the sacred ground of your creation, O God.
You are always there before us.
You are always there beside us.
You will walk the way ahead of us.
Bless, we pray, the sacred ground of the world
where we live and work.**

We place this earth in the bowl
and we name our sacred ground before our God:

The people name the places where they live

We remember other places around the world
which is also your sacred ground:

The people name the places

Be revealed there, O God.
**Show us the power of your justice, love and peace.
Amen.**

SONG

Go into this day in faith.
And may every step you take,
and every moment of living and moving,
be blessed as though you walk with God.
Amen.

TURN AWAY FROM DEATH

GREETING

The peace of Christ be with you!
And also with you.

CALL TO WORSHIP

God is creating new things!
Before they break forth from the bud,
God has announced them.
Turn away from death!

Christ is walking towards all that defeats us,
walking towards life that will never die.
Turn away from death!

The Spirit of God, like fire, like wind,
lifts us, turns us and calls us on
in an eternal passion for life.
Turn away from death!
Let us worship God.

SONG

WE ARE STILL ATTRACTED TO DEATH

We confess that death still has its attractions for us, O God.
It sometimes feels more comfortable,
more safe,
and less costly.

Silent reflection

We mostly recognize the more dramatic deaths,
like crucifying people, and like the traumatic deaths
which we experience at the hands of others, O God.
But it's harder to see the deaths
in the times when we do nothing, O God,
when we don't care enough,
don't share things justly
and remain silent in the face of suffering.

Silent reflection

Forgive us, God of life.
Forgive us, God of love,
and turn us around towards your life.

ASSURANCE OF PARDON
The word to us in Christ
is that Jesus walks on in courage towards our deaths,
forgiving us as he goes and ending the power of death.
Thanks be to God!

READINGS
Isaiah 55.1–9
1 Corinthians 10.1–13

SONG

THE GOSPEL
Luke 13.1–9

SERMON

AFFIRMATION OF FAITH
In response to the word, let us stand and affirm our faith:

We believe that death is real,
that within our life we can destroy ourselves
and the life in others.
We believe that new life is possible,
and that it can be created
and recreated by God.
This we believe.

We believe that life is more powerful than death,
that, in Jesus,
we see love that could not be defeated,
justice that refused to lay down its dream,
courage that stood beyond its weakness
and hope that defied every despair.
This we believe.

We believe that life
dances on in the power of the Spirit,
singing songs of universal joy,
leaping past us in its freedoms
and calling us on into life.
This we believe.
Christ has died.
Christ is risen.
Christ will come again.

PRAYERS OF INTERCESSION

Let us share, before God,
the fruits of life for which we long,
the situations which we would like to see change,
and the changes we hope for in ourselves.

The people share these longings

Take our longings and hopes, O God,
and nurture our life
that we may be those
who live in fruitfulness
with each other and the world.
Amen.

SONG

BLESSING

Go in peace,
And may the holy God be revealed in surprising life,
Christ Jesus turn you around towards new possibilities
and the Spirit be your company on the way.
Amen.

TENANTS IN GOD'S HOUSEHOLD
For a time of review

For this service you will need

• *Symbols of parish life and activities*

GREETING

Today we place the life of this congregation before God.
Here we symbolize our life together.

Symbols of parish life are placed on the table

Here we wait to know more than we know now.

CALL TO WORSHIP

We come with open hearts to hear the voice of God,
singing through our songs,
breathing the word into our silences,
challenging us in our speaking and listening
and calling to God's people down the ages.
Let us worship God!

PRAYER OF INVOCATION

You are always with us, God of eternity,
but we pray that we will find you here
in the mystery of this hour.
Come to us, loving One,
come to us, Jesus Christ, come, Holy Spirit,
for we long to know you more.
None of us will ever know all of you,
because you are beyond our knowing, Holy God.
But as you spoke to the people of Israel,
as you walked with the first disciples
and because you have told us you will never leave us alone,
we wait to discover your presence among us here.
We pray this in faith.
Amen.

SONG

PRAYER OF CONFESSION

Dear God, as we become aware of your goodness,
we are only too aware that we have often failed.
We listen to you speaking to your people through the biblical
   witnesses
and we wonder if we have even paused to wait for your word to us.

Silent reflection

As the tenants in your household,
we look with concern at our life together
and our life with those around us,
and we ask ourselves whether we are really the people you hoped
   we would be.

Silent reflection

Have we created a community here which you could safely enter
if you came to us today?
Have we made a cherishing place here for the little and the least,
the people whom you so love?

Silent reflection

Forgive us, loving God.
Forgive us and make us your community of grace.
Amen.

WORDS OF ASSURANCE

Hear the word of hope in Jesus Christ:
Nothing in all creation can separate us from the love of God in
   Christ Jesus.
We are forgiven!
Thanks be to God!

READINGS

Exodus 20.1–4, 7–9, 12–20
Psalm 19
Philippians 3.4b–14

SONG

THE GOSPEL

Matthew 21.33–42

SERMON

SONG

PRAYER OF THANKSGIVING

We thank you, God, that you do not leave us without the word.
It comes to us from those who struggled to understand the way
of truth
down the centuries and we thank you that you are still moving
among us,
bringing us new understandings of truth.
Speak to us now, that we may live.
Amen.

OFFERING PRAYER

God of generosity and kindness,
we will never be able to match your open heart,
but we pray that you will take what we have given and add to it
your own gifts of love.
Amen.

PRAYERS OF INTERCESSION

For whom will we pray, O God?
For what will we pray?
The world swirls around us in its pain and need.
Our church struggles to know what to do in response to that.
Maybe if we remain silent before you,
your wise Spirit will pray for us?

A silence is kept

Come to us and make your way clearer to us, O Spirit of truth.
Come down your holy mountain, O God.
Come down your holy mountain, O God.

Draw near to your world in its warfare and woundedness.
Draw near to those who struggle to survive.
Draw near to those who are lonely and afraid.
These are the people whom we remember before you:

The people add their prayers for specific people

Draw near to your church in its frailty and wandering from
your way.

Draw near to us and challenge us if we have fenced in your love
and kept it to ourselves.
Expand our vision so that the world will see the light of your life
among us.
Come down your holy mountain, O God.
Come down your holy mountain, O God.

Draw near to each one of us today, O God who sees and cares,
reach out towards us and speak tenderly to us,
that we may discover your life of hope and courage closer than
we had ever imagined.
Take all our humble efforts here and add to them your truth
and grace.
Come down your holy mountain, O God.
Come down your holy mountain, O God.
For we ask this in faith,
Amen.

COMMISSIONING AND BLESSING

Go forth, faithful tenants of God's household!
The world is waiting for us.
The world is longing for those who bring in God's order of truth
and love.
Go forth as those who see and hear a new word for this day.
And may God be experienced beside us,
a rock from the mountain of holiness,
a tree of life in which you may find a nesting place,
and a landscape of freedom and peace.
Amen.

INVITED TO THE FEAST

CALL TO WORSHIP

We are the people invited, invited to the feast of God:
Come in humble faith.

Today is the day of the feast, we will not wait until tomorrow:
Come in humble faith.

The communion elements are placed on the table

Today is the day of our salvation, the day of grace:
Come in humble faith to worship God.

PRAYER OF INVOCATION

God, who invites us to come towards you,
we pray that you will come towards us,
that we may know who we are and whose we are.
Be present with us now as we gather here,
hoping, believing, that we are called to your wedding feast.
Stay with us, O God, and stay with those who long to be with us.
Amen.

CONFESSION

God, whose costly life in the world often challenges our small ideas
about what it means to be your people,
we make our confession before you.
If we have become so engrossed in many activities
that it is a long time since we stopped
and asked whether our gods are now false gods:
Forgive us, O God.
Forgive us, O God.

A silence is kept

If we are so confident of our place at your table
that we have not searched our lives
to see whether we are excluding the very people who need you most:
Forgive us, O God.
Forgive us, O God.

A silence is kept

If we refuse to enter the banquet
because we cannot imagine that we could share
in your celebration of life,
rejecting your offer of forgiveness for the past,
and your kind invitation to be present now with you:
Forgive us, O God.
Forgive us, O God.

WORDS OF ASSURANCE

Even while we are yet sinners,
the word to us in Christ Jesus is that we are loved of God,
called again and again into God's forgiveness and grace.
Receive the forgiveness of God!
Amen.

READINGS

Exodus 32.1–14
Psalm 106.1–6, 19–23
Philippians 4.1–9
Matthew 22.1–14

PRAYER OF THANKSGIVING

O God, who longs for us to be part of the wonders of the
    wedding banquet,
who prepares for us overflowing gifts,
we thank you that your love reaches far beyond our imagining.
We thank you that sometimes,
just when we believe that we are outside the feast,
you invite us in and seat us at your table of joy.
Thank you, God, thank you for that.
Amen.

PRAYERS OF INTERCESSION

In covenant with you, O God, who never betrays us,
we come in humble prayer to ask for your help.
We would be your people, as you are our God.
Please, dear God, share with us in the task
of opening the feast of heaven to all those you love.
These are the people who we have seen receiving less of the feast
    of life.

The people share their prayers for others

Hear our prayers, O God.
For we pray in faith.

We pray for your church, O God, who never leaves us alone.
Expand our faithfulness,
lift up new hope among us,
create here a community which can be seen by others

as your wedding banquet, full of committed love,
spreading before the world a joyful generosity
with unexpected gifts and laughter,
and openness of heart and soul.

Silent prayer

Hear our prayers, O God.
For we pray in faith.

We pray for ourselves, O God of our being,
stir within our fenced-off fears,
move boldly within our boundaries for life
that we may see the bright vision of your hope for us
and set our feet towards the riches of your promises.

Silent prayer

Hear our prayers, O God.
For we pray in faith.

Come to us, the One who brings grace upon grace,
in the name of Jesus Christ,
Amen.

THE EUCHARIST

COMMISSIONING AND BLESSING

We are the guests at God's banquet.
Let us enter the sacred life of Jesus Christ, who is the Way,
    the Truth and the Life,
clad in the robes of the Holy Spirit as the garments of celebration
and treading on the holy ground of the Creator.
May the delights of the feast of God lie before us,
the door to grace be wide open in all that we do
and the Spirit take us by the hand in welcome.
Amen.

Needing Support

The ears of our God are tuned to all of us,
never missing the fragile voices or whispers of desperation,
hearing the messages within our messages,
listening for the silent sounds of longing,
choosing the crying voices from within the louder sounds,
lifting up the voices of humanness,
the voices of caring,
the voices of the little and the least.

JUST WALKING BY
Moments for good Samaritans

For this service you will need

- *A basket of stones and dead leaves*
- *A cloth to represent a road*
- *A cross in a central place*

GREETING
The peace of Christ be with you.
And also with you.

OPENING SENTENCES
The world lies by the roadside in its weeping struggling life:
and you stop and live in its pain, Jesus Christ.

We sit on the edge of the road in rejection and fear:
**and you join us as though we are your dear neighbours,
  Jesus Christ.**

There is no place separated from your love.
There is no time when you pass us by.
Thanks be to God!

SONG

AS WE WERE WALKING BY
As we were walking by our neighbours, O God,
we were afraid to stop in case they asked too much of us.

Silent prayer

As we passed some other neighbours, O God,
we were afraid to stop because people might think we were
  like them.

Silent prayer

As we sat on the other side of the room from our neighbours,
    O God,
we could not believe that they had any good within them or love
    for us
and so we did not look for their good, or receive love from them.

Silent prayer

Forgive us, gracious God.
Forgive us and wait with us as we see our neighbours again.

ASSURANCE OF PARDON

In Jesus Christ, our God never walks past those who fail.
Even the wounds of our wrongdoings are bathed and offered
    God's healing love.
From the Spirit have we all received, grace upon grace.
Amen.

READINGS
Amos 7.7–17
Colossians 1.1–14

SONG

THE GOSPEL
Luke 10.25–37

SERMON

AFFIRMATION OF FAITH

In response to the word, let us stand and affirm our faith:

The mind of our God is wiser than our minds,
searching among the depths of our life
with all its ambiguity and fears,
all its complex wanderings and lack of understanding,
cutting through to truth
and the lost grounds of justice.

The ears of our God are tuned to all of us,
never missing fragile voices or whispers of desperation,
hearing the messages within our messages,
listening for the silent sounds of longing,
choosing the crying voices from within the louder sounds,
lifting up the voices of humanness,
the voices of caring,
the voices of the little and the least.

The heart of our God feels for us,
carrying the feet of the Christ into the world,
to know the way of our wilderness,
a heart filled with costly love,
a heart which reaches out to touch us all
and spreads its love with the balm of healing,
lifting us to our feet and carrying us to a safe place
before we travel the road of life again.

We believe in a God
who is neighbour to us all.

SONG

PRAYERS OF THE PEOPLE
Neighbour God,
open our eyes to see our neighbours at this time,
those who lie beside the roadside of our life,
like unnoticed stones or dead leaves.
Open our eyes to see who are our neighbours now.

Silent reflection as a basket of stones and dead leaves is placed

The cloth of compassion streams towards our life from the cross.

A cloth is spread from the cross onto the floor towards the people

Let us name our wounded neighbours,
see their life as a rock or the dead leaf by the roadside
and place it gently on the cloth of compassion.

The people name the neighbours and place the stones and leaves

Let us cover the wounds of our neighbours.

The cloth of compassion is tenderly curled over the stones and leaves

Bind up all our wounds, O God.
Make us neighbours to all who need neighbours.
Give us humble souls to recognize in others
the gift of being neighbours to us.
Amen.

SONG

BLESSING
Go onto the road of life in kindness,
and may Jesus be walking by your wounds
and stop to carry you into healing,
and may the God of love and the Spirit of grace
flow forth in all you do.
Amen.

SURVIVAL OF THE
VULNERABLE GOOD
The flight into Egypt

For this service you will need

- *Small candles and tapers to light them*

OPENING SENTENCES
Love has come.
Love has come among us, even us,
risking its own destruction:
God with us.
God for us all.

Grace lies here in frailty.
Grace has come among us, even us,
journeying through costly pathways:
God with us.
God for us all.

MUSIC

CONFESSION
O God, we see the things of hope, of love and justice,
of peace and truth, in ourselves and in our world,
in fearful battle with the powerful forces
which would defeat and destroy them.

A silence is kept

If we have lost faith that they will survive:
Forgive us.

When we hand them over to the tyrants of our day,
without much struggle:
Forgive us.

If we have given up hope in precious parts of ourselves:
Forgive us.

ASSURANCE
Hear the word of assurance:
life is stronger than death in us.
Christ is come.
Love is cherished in the hand of God.
Thanks be to God.

READING
Matthew 2.13–23

REFLECTION

AFFIRMATION
How will we believe, O God?
And yet we will,
and yet we must,
or nothing is possible beyond what we can now see.
Let us affirm our faith together:

We believe,
against all our realities
and the lack of hope around us,

we believe in God.
**We believe that Jesus Christ
and the life of this Christ will survive in the world.
We believe that the Spirit is still with us,
the Spirit of God, the Spirit of Christ.
We believe that we are eternally linked
with the love and good and courage of our God,
if we will choose to be.
And we so choose.**

PRAYERS

Let us light a candle for each fragile cause,
for each vulnerable person we know
who needs to be carried to safety, cherished in the arms of God.

Small candles are placed in the centre and the people light them

Our hopes and our faith are like these very small lights,
flickering in the wind of life as they travel along unknown ways,
like Mary and Joseph carrying the Christchild to safety.
We pray, O God, that these people will be kept safe.
**We will share in the holding of their life.
We will share in the carrying of courage and faith
    alongside them.
Be with us as we go, God of our journey.
In the name of the Christ,
Amen.**

MUSIC

BLESSING

Go in peace,
and may the God who protected the Holy Child
cover you and keep you,
the God who came to be with us be found beside you,
and the love within you be called into safe places
by the gentle Spirit.
Amen.

IT'S NOT EASY

For this service you will need

- *A many-coloured cloth*
- *A long purple cloth*
- *A cross*

CALL TO WORSHIP

We are the people of dignity,
our many-coloured lives stretched out before us:
with a God who sets us free.

A many-coloured cloth is placed on the table

We are the people with awesome choices:
with a God who walks before us on the way.

A long purple cloth is placed across the coloured cloth

We are the people called to live in fullness of life:
with a God who loves us to the death.

A cross is placed at the head of the purple cloth

Let us worship God.

PRAYER OF INVOCATION

Be with us in every moment of this service, O God, who knows
   all that faces us.
Be with us in our praying, our singing and as we speak and
   listen to your word for us.
Be with us, God, who is like a mother hen who gathers us under
   her warm wings.
Be with us in Spirit and in truth.
Amen.

SONG

CONFESSION

How do we know what you want us to do, O God?
Sometimes there are more questions than answers
and we cannot decide what is due to you and how that is to
   be delivered to you.

We confess that sometimes it is easier to do what others ask of us.
In your mercy:
Forgive us, O God.

If we have listened to the loudest voices asking for our support,
or the ones which suit us best and ask least of us,
in your mercy:
Forgive us, O God.

Silent reflection

If we have given more loyalty to earthly rulers
than to your still small voice with us
and others have suffered because of this,
in your mercy:
Forgive us, O God.

When we crush the prophetic among us
because we do not want to hear the costly truth
and your call to give our due to you,
in your mercy:
Forgive us, O God.

For we ask this in Christ's name,
Amen.

ASSURANCE
Receive in faith the forgiveness of Jesus Christ, who was tempted
like us to bow down to the authority of the powers of ego, of
applause and of seductive evil forces.
We are forgiven!
Thanks be to God.

READINGS
Exodus 33.12–23
1 Thessalonians 1.1–10
Matthew 22.15–22

SERMON

SONG

PRAYER OF INTERCESSION
O God, who has given us the dignity of free choice,

we often long for your wisdom
in discerning where the authority of Caesar and that of God
    begins and ends.
Life is sometimes very complicated
and we feel powerless to make a difference
when we are confronted by the power of Caesar.
Sometimes we think that the powers and principalities of our day
really do separate us from your love in Christ Jesus.

Silent prayer

We pray that your mind will become clearer to us,
that we will not shrink from the hard decisions
and that we will encourage each other more in doing that.

Silent prayer

There are many longings in our hearts as we remember the task
    before us.

The people share their longings

Come to us, Spirit of wisdom,
be present in our midst, Spirit of truth,
rise again, life of Christ before us,
with your wounded hands outstretched
and linked with the suffering people of the world,
that we may be strengthened
to challenge all that stands between us and your will for the world.
This we pray,
for Christ's sake
Amen.

SONG

COMMISSIONING AND BLESSING
Be bold in the claiming of the gospel for the whole creation.
Be brave in the lifting up of the life of God in every place.
Be firm in carrying the holy name of Jesus Christ into the
    palaces of worldly power.
Be gentle in the understanding of ourselves and one another.
And may the songs of the Creator sound with love in all the earth,
the tenderness of Christ Jesus cover the wounds of the people
and the truth in the Holy Spirit rise free in every age.
Amen.

SERVICE OF PRAYER AND CONCERN FOR OUTWORKERS
For a religious setting

This service was prepared for an action group (FairWear) that supports the struggle for justice of women employed as textile workers, mostly in their own homes. Their pay is well below average and they are often forced to work in 'sweatshop' conditions. Those who benefit from their work charge top prices for the garments they produce, often under well-known fashionable labels. It is included in this book as an idea which may be adapted to relate to other situations of oppression and injustice.

Preparation

Ask those likely to attend to bring with them a label taken from an item of (Australian-made) clothing. Obtain a length of cloth (about 3 metres – purple if possible). If appropriate, encourage people to have tea or coffee after the service and to write letters together.

OPENING SENTENCES

The God of love opens our eyes to see the suffering of the people:
And we will see.

The God of justice opens our ears to hear those who cry out:
And we will hear.

In the power of the Spirit, we will know the truth:
And the truth will set us free.

SONG

CONFESSION
It is hard to see and hear and know the truth about injustice.

Voice 1:
We have created societies where money is more important than people.
God, forgive us.

Voice 2:
We look at the images of glamorous models
rather than the worn-out lives of those who make their clothes.
God, forgive us.

Voice 3:
We choose to forget the cost in the lives of outworkers for the
bargains we buy.
God, forgive us.

ASSURANCE

Today is a new day! Rise up and live with justice and love in the
power of Christ.
Amen!

READINGS

Suggested:
Isaiah 58.6–12
Isaiah 25.1–10
Micah 6.1–8
Psalm 96
Luke 1.46–55
James 5.4

STORIES FROM THE WOMEN AND/OR SPEAKER

OUR RESPONSE

This is the stretched-out life of a woman outworker.

*Two people stretch out the purple cloth across a table and down onto the
floor*

Let us look at this cloth and imagine what her life might be like.

Voice 1:
She is tired, committed to her family, who probably also work too
hard.

Voice 2:
She is afraid of her employer because she might lose her work.

Voice 3:
She is skilled and faithful.

Voice 4:
She is a person of dignity and loved by God.
Are there other words we would say about her life?

People add words

The labels we have brought are the sign that she has finished this
   piece of work.
They are our connection with her life.
They may tell us, if we wish to know,
how fairly she has been paid for this work which we now receive.
Let us place our labels on the edge of her life.

The people place their labels on the end of the cloth

Let us make our commitment:
**We commit ourselves to search for the truth about injustice
and to act in response to that knowledge.
We will not knowingly buy clothes which are the products
   of exploitation.
We will stand with outworkers in their struggle
and challenge those who are their oppressors.**

We will send these labels to the FairWear office as a sign of our
joining with others in a commitment to justice for the outworkers
of Australia and beyond.

PRAYERS

We pray for all outworkers who are exploited, exhausted, or harassed,
who receive none of the work entitlements which we take for granted:
And we celebrate their growing empowerment.

We pray for those who struggle for justice alongside the outworkers,
their unions, Asian Women at Work, FairWear and other advocates:
And we celebrate their energy, courage and wisdom.

We pray for all employers of outworkers, for governments and policy
makers:
And we celebrate those who are ethical, caring and just.

We pray for ourselves, that we may be part of the transformation of
the world:
**And we celebrate the Good News which we find among us.
Amen.**

SONG

BLESSING
Go in faith to renew the whole creation.
And may the goodness of God's creation
be found in the little and the least,
Christ be present in the longings in the face of our neighbour,
and the Spirit show us the way towards true peace.
Amen.

FOR THE UPROOTED ONES
Remembering refugees

For this service you will need

- *A large map of the world*
- *Flowers or ribbons or small candles*

CALL TO WORSHIP
There is no place where you cannot reach:
God who made the heavens and the earth.

There is no journey which you have not travelled:
God who shared our life in Jesus Christ.

There are no people beyond your care:
God who is the Spirit, the Comforter.
Let us worship God!

SONG

GATHER THEM IN
Let us 'gather in' to our community of faith
some of the people who are uprooted
from their homes and countries around the world.

The names of countries where there are known to be refugees are read and flowers are placed on the table for them, or candles lit, or a ribbon attached to the map is linked with the congregation or the communion table

As we gather together in this place,
we remember these people and the struggle of their lives.
We will remember them before our God.

IT IS NOT EASY TO WELCOME EVERYONE

Even when we hope we can do better,
it is not easy to welcome everyone who wants to live among us,
or needs our prayers and concerned support, O God.
There are many reasons why we find it hard.

The people say why it is hard

Or:

Voice 1:
Sometimes we feel people are very different from us,
in culture, in looks, in ways of relating, in their politics, in their religion.

Voice 2:
Or we feel as though there is not enough
to share with them in work, in houses, in schools, in money, in services.

Voice 3:
Sometimes we are tired
and cannot find the energy to give the care,
or the time that they may hope from us,
especially when they are far away.
Forgive us, O God, if we have been less than generous.
We remember your grace in relating to us
and we long to be as gracious to others.

ASSURANCE

Our prayers are heard.
We too are gathered into the love of God.
Thanks be to God!

READINGS

SONG

SERMON

AFFIRMATION OF FAITH

In response to the word, let us stand and affirm our faith:

**We are all held in the hollow of God's hand,
loved children of the universe,
born from the life which flows from God,
freed to the fullness of God's creation
with all its beauty and variety.**

**We are all worth dying for in Christ Jesus,
all called to risen life in Christ's rising.
The way of Jesus gives us footprints for our following
and all our trials and longings are known
in the frailty of Christ's birth among us
and the courage of Christ's walking with us.**

**We are all called to new things in the Spirit,
in the hope that stirs in unlikely moments,
the home we find in the wastelands of our wanderings,
the warmth that we touch in the coldness of our need
and the opening of our hearts to adventures in belonging
or the gathering in of those without a home.**

THE OFFERING IS RECEIVED

Dear God, receive our offering.
Guide those who use it, that it may help to bring fullness of life
to those who live in need and long for our care.
Amen.

INTERCESSION

As they face this day, O God, find those who are lost,
separated from those they love,
crossing unknown borders,
without a country or home,
not knowing where to turn:
**Find them, God who always seeks for the lost,
and cover them safely as a hen covers her chickens.**

As they face this day, O God,
stand among the ones in refugee camps around the world,
in the hunger and despair,
in the crowds and the emptiness,
in the wet and the thirstiness:
Be their hope and their strength
in the crying out for justice
and open the ears of the world to hear their cries.

As they face this day, O God,
may those who live with us, uprooted from their homelands,
find a new home where their history is respected,
their gifts and graces celebrated
and their fear departed from them.
May we be their home,
may we be the ones who open our hearts in welcome.

As we face this day, O God,
sing to us your song of encouragement,
paint for us your bright pictures of a new world
where people need not flee from wars and oppression,
where no one lacks a country or a home,
and where we are all part of your new creation.
For we long to be your people, in spirit and in truth.
We pray in the name of Jesus the Christ,
who knew the life of a refugee.
Amen.

THE LORD'S PRAYER

SONG

BLESSING AND DISMISSAL
Go in peace and grace.
And may God lift up new possibilities before us,
the face of Christ be seen in our neighbours
and the Spirit lead us into the celebration of a new community.
Amen.

With the Wider Community

We commit ourselves to search for the truth about injustice
and to act in response to that knowledge.
We will not knowingly participate in exploitation.
We will stand with the people in their struggle
and challenge those who are their oppressors.

MISSING PERSONS

This introduction and prayer was created to close Missing Persons Week in the state of New South Wales in Australia. It was a week where the community focused its care both on those who were missing and those who suffered the loss of their disappearance.

OPENING

This has been a week when we as members of the community have been invited to remember that in our midst are a whole group of people who live with unresolved and mostly unrecognized grief because their family member or friend has disappeared.

We have been invited to realize that also in our midst is often hidden the answer to the questions that lie within that disappearance.

- Sometimes the answers are about the disappeared person living unknown and unnamed among us with all the complex reasons for that.
- Sometimes the answers are about hidden violence, abuse and destruction that have never been faced or made visible in this, our life together.

You who have lost the ones you love into a mystery of silence and emptiness face a hard journey into the future.

- How can you lay those missing loved ones to rest if it is still possible that you should be calling them more loudly towards life and love from you?
- Will you betray them and your love for them if you stop hoping to reconnect with their life?
- Was there something you should have done?
- Is there something more you should be doing now?

In the many crises and traumas in life, in the face of things that it seems we cannot change or really understand, often our best refuge and comfort is to place ourselves and those we love out into a wider community of life than our own and to respect our own small efforts as being enough.

In respecting our own efforts to live as best we can we can say to ourselves:

We are not God.
We are ordinary homely human beings and at each point in our lives we have done what we could.
We will rest with that and honour our own humble human journeys as significant.

If who we are and what we have done or not done has impacted on the life of others, we ask their forgiveness and the forgiveness of God.

We will walk into the future accepting our ordinary selves and giving all our energy into the future rather than into the past.

We will honour the past by carrying with us, very close to our hearts, our real and ongoing love for the things we have lost and the ones we have lost.

In placing our lives onto a wider space for healing and hope:

We ask that you see this grieving that we carry with us and gather around us the caring and respect that we need to journey on.

We ask you to share the burden of looking for the lost ones so that we do not feel the whole burden is ours.

We ask you to see if, in the midst of this our community, you can participate with us in creating a safer and more loving place for all people so that, if they go missing,

- you will all ask why;
- you will all assume responsibility for finding the lost;
- and you will not forget that this is happening among us.

That is why this week has been important for us all.
It is your way of inviting these things from us.
On behalf of the part of the community which cares about that, I can only say that we have heard.
With great respect and concern, we honour your loss and your grieving and we share your pain now and into the future.

Let us gather the elements around us and those we have lost:

Let us hear the rain and see it creating rivers around our feet.

As we listen, let us imagine that even the heavens are joining their tears with ours as we grieve for those who are lost and that the rivers around our feet are joined with the rivers of the tears which have been shed.

Then let us remember that the very rain that we hear and see will join with the sun and produce the flowers around us in the spring, the greening of the trees and the earth – that from the tears may come new life and hope blossoming forth.

As we feel the breath of the wind, let us imagine that it blows our love towards our loved ones, wherever they are.

I have been asked to say a prayer:

Dear God, nothing is hidden from you.
You see all that is to be seen.
You know all that is to be known.
You understand all that is a mystery to us.

If those we love are still living,
search for them like you searched for the one sheep who is lost.
Call to their hearts in your voice of love,
a voice full of understanding of all difficult and complex journeys,
and bring our loved ones home to us.
Give to them a message of hope about our love and longing
    for them,
so that they may come to us without fear and with trust.
O God, bring them home if they can come.
O God, keep them safe and happy, if they will not come,
and give us peace in believing that we can live with their decision.

O God, if they are not now living,
gather their lives which are lost to us into the safety of your
    loving arms.
Take these our children, our wives and husbands,
our mothers and fathers and friends,
these our precious lost ones,
and tell them that we know they have been lost to us,
that we grieve them still,
that there are many things of love and truth that we wanted
    to say to them,
many acts of kindness and grace that are missing between us.
Love them, O God, as we would have gone on loving them.

Heal them if they have been hurt and cherish them if they
   have left us in fear and pain.

Give us your peace on this day and in all our next days.
Surround us with the care of those who know us,
and give us the wisdom, love and strength to make a place here for
   all people that is safe, compassionate, just and free from violence.
Amen.

Let us go from here in peace.

HONOURING THE OUTWORKERS
A ritual for use in a secular setting

*This is focused on the outworkers in the textile industry in Australia but
could be adapted for use with other groups who suffer injustice in the
workplace. Preparation is as for the Service of Prayer and Concern on
page 96.*

OPENING
Outworkers are people worthy of being honoured.
Their lives are significant.
Their cause is just.
Let us mark their struggle by pausing and remembering them.

MUSIC

WE WOULD LIKE TO DO MORE
It is hard to see and hear and know the truth about injustice.

Voice 1:
We have created societies where money is more important than people.

Silent reflection

Voice 2:
We look at the images of glamorous models
rather than the worn-out lives of those who make their clothes.

Silent reflection

Voice 3:
We choose to forget the cost in the lives of outworkers for the
bargains we buy.

Silent reflection

But we will do more.
We can do more.
Yes, we will and we can!

STORIES FROM THE WOMEN AND/OR SPEAKER

OUR RESPONSE
This is the stretched-out life of a woman outworker.

*Two people stretch out a purple cloth across a table and down onto the
floor*

Let us look at this cloth and imagine what her life might be like.

Voice 1:
She is tired, and committed to her family.

Voice 2:
She is afraid of her employer because she might lose her work.

Voice 3:
She is skilled and faithful.

Voice 4:
She is a person of dignity.
Are there other words we would say about her life?

People add words

The labels we have brought are the sign that she has finished this
    piece of work.
They are our connection with her life.
They may tell us, if we wish to know,
how fairly she has been paid for this work which we now receive.
Let us place our labels on the edge of her life.

The people place their labels on the end of the cloth

Let us make our commitment:
**We commit ourselves to search for the truth about injustice
and to act in response to that knowledge.
We will not knowingly buy clothes which are the products of
exploitation.
We will stand with outworkers in their struggle
and challenge those who are their oppressors.**

SHARING OUR STRENGTH AND HOPE

At this moment we offer our hope and strength to all outworkers
who are exploited, exhausted, or harassed,
who receive none of the work entitlements which we take for granted:
We celebrate their growing empowerment.

We share our hope and strength with those who struggle for justice
alongside the outworkers, the Textile, Clothing and Footwear Union,
FairWear, Asian Women at Work, and other advocates:
We celebrate their energy, courage and commitment.

We support all employers of outworkers, industry bodies,
governments and policy makers who are moving towards justice:
We celebrate those who are ethical, caring and just.

We have hope in the Industrial Relations Commission
as it decides on awards and conditions for working people:
**We celebrate its existence and the moments
when it is the voice for the rights of the people.**

We share hope and energy with each other, that we may be creative
agents of change:
We celebrate that this is indeed possible.

LET US GO OUT

Let us go out into the world,
determined to make it a different place for all people.
Let us stand in solidarity with the outworkers
until justice is done.
So be it!

MUSIC

— 110 —

Occasional Prayers

Give us the faith to believe
that this is the pathway through to life.
You, who spent time in the wilderness,
remember with us your struggling.
You, who were tossed in the centre of storms,
remember with us the fear of that moment.
You, whose friends slept through your agony of heart,
remember with us the loneliness.

CALL TO US, SPIRIT OF GOD

As we tread the ground of this place,
call to us, Spirit of God.
Open our ears to hear the sound of your voice
speaking into the desert silences,
stirring in the moving
of the bushland trees,
singing songs in the rhythm of our farm life
and rising free in the humming of our cities.

Call to us again, Spirit of God.
Make your music of peace and joy
in the midst of our life.
For your song is true,
your voice is of love
and in your Holy Spirit lies our hope.
Amen.

MOVING WITH YOUR SPIRIT IS NOT ALWAYS EASY

Dear God,
moving with your Spirit is not always easy.
The way forward
is not as clear as we would like it to be.
It sometimes feels safer to stay where we are,
and then the ground goes from under our feet
and we know that we have no option but to move.

Give us love for each other on the way, O God.
Show us your footsteps on the path, Jesus Christ,
and hold us safe as we go, Holy Spirit,
who is our comforter, our grace,
and the one who prays for us,
even as we cannot find the words.
Amen.

SOMETIMES WE THINK WE ARE SMALL GODS

Sometimes we think we are small gods,
God of all creation.
We think we own this land
and can tame its eternal energies.
But it teaches us who we are in the cosmos, O God.
Its endless changing rhythms
of flood and dryness,
fire and fertility,
invite us, age by age,
to simply take our place
as your humble children,
thankfully receiving small and larger gifts,
invited to cherish a mysterious landscape
of your making.
In deep respect, we give our thanks.
Amen.

THERE IS A GRIEVING

Sometimes there is a grieving in our hearts,
God of understanding.
Our lives enter the agony of the turmoil,
the search for your truth.
We wonder why others cannot see its clarity
like we do.
And then we look upon their faces
and see the pain of a different conviction.

Surely you could give us a sign, O God?
Surely you could save us from this distress?
Surely you could take this cup from us?

If we must drink it for our journeying,
please give to us a wine of kindness,
give to us a poured forth grace
and the nourishing power of your Spirit
for our survival together.
Amen.

WHAT IS YOUR HOPE FOR US, GOD?

What is your hope, O God?
It is not always clear to us.

We long for a safe place
where we can look upon your face
and you seem to offer us
a track through a wilderness.

Give us the faith to believe
that this is the pathway through to life.
You, who spent time in a wilderness,
remember with us your struggling.
You, who were tossed in the centre of storms,
remember with us the fear of that moment.
You, whose friends slept through your agony of heart,
remember with us the loneliness.

Please, O God, make straight the path before us.
Calm the storm in the midst of our life together
and take our hand for the next step of the way.
Amen.

THERE IS JOY

Dear God, there is a joy
deep within our heart,
the joy of trusting
in one who has been this way before us,
the wonder of the mystery of your love
for homely people like us,
and for the waking to a day
in which you always promise
new possibilities.
Thank you for this day.
Amen.

SET US DOWN

Set us down in our true place, O God,
as precious people
among the height, breadth and depth of your creation.
Set us down among the miracle of your church,
surviving in a thousand places,
in a thousand, thousand moments,
with its face turned in hope and faith
towards your love.
Set us down in the marvels of your universe,

with its interdependent patterns
of complex life.
Set us down as unique players
in a long history
of your longing for a world
of right relationships
and resurrection life.
Amen.

IS THIS GOD REALLY WISE?

There is a God,
who comes to us as wisdom,
but is this God really wise?

Here we are, O God,
down in this deep dark pit of struggle,
of lack of hope and faith as we look at our life,
and there you are beside us, among us and around us,
joining our weeping, our angry protest
and the burden of our journeying.
Is this wise?

This, our God, joins us
with arms wide open and bleeding hands
and wounded side,
nailed to a cross.

What sort of wisdom do you offer to us, O Jesus Christ?

Silent reflection

How can it be that your pain
absorbs our own?
And yet it might,
if we wait upon the moment in hope.
Amen.

A CALLING TO FAITH

Dear God, we look out into our world
and we wonder if it is possible to have faith.

We see the powerful oppressors
run rough-shod over the suffering people.

We see the refugees fleeing their borders
year after year.
We see the might of violence win
in the face of peacefulness and love.
We see our own small efforts for change
apparently come to less than nothing.

Dear God, we believe.
help us in our unbelief.

Sometimes we would rather not know any more
about the pain of the world,
in case it stretches our faith to breaking point.
And then, we remember those who live the suffering,
who cannot escape the oppression,
whose bodies bear the violence
and who have less power than we do.
We are called to faith again,
because they, our sisters and brothers,
cry out to us and call us on.

Dear God, we believe.
Help us in our unbelief.
Amen.

COME TO THE FEAST

Was it a wedding, or the feast of heaven
that all those people were invited to, O God?
They made all the excuses in the world
so you feasted with the people
from the highways and byways instead.

It is hard for us to imagine refusing your invitation, O God.
But then we have seen the resurrection.
We have seen that Jesus is the Christ.
We have formed your church.

We are always there for Christmas and Easter,
For Lent, Advent and Pentecost.
Our lives are full in our preparations for them.
Our money is given to sustain them
and all the things that are part of them.

We have built you a beautiful altar
and surrounded it with stained-glass windows.
Our music and singing rises in your praise.

So, who are these people from the highways and byways
who haunt us with their crying out
for food and shelter and freedom?

Silent reflection

Have mercy on us, O God.
Have mercy on us, Jesus Christ.
Call us to the real feast of life, Holy Spirit.
Amen.

PRAISE BE TO GOD!

Praise be to God,
who calls the people to new hope in every generation,
who lifts our eyes to see a new heaven and a new earth
which one day will break through the old, tired efforts
and reach into justice beyond our imagining.

Praise be to God,
who leads us on past crucifixions of failure,
rejection and faithlessness,
drawing a picture of a world ready to blossom from the bud,
delicate and fragile,
vulnerable as a baby in Bethlehem.

Praise be to God,
who brings to life the dead bodies of despair
which lie entombed in our souls
and in our churches,
dancing ahead of us undefeated
in the Spirit of truth and healing and love.
Praise be to God!
Amen.

GOD IN THE DEATHS

Are you a God who travels most vividly in deaths?

The death of trying to earn my salvation
in the risk of receiving the free gift of abundant life?